North Norfolk's Wildlife

Discovering its birds and natural history

Andrew Bloomfield and Gary Smith

Red String Publishing

Andrew Bloomfield dedicates this book to his family - Emma, Angus and Grace

Gary Smith dedicates this book to Maggie

Early marsh orchid of the form coccinea

Published by Red String Publishing
20 Lancaster Road
Blenheim Park
Sculthorpe
Fakenham
Norfolk
NR21 7PX
www.northnorfolkwildlife.co.uk

ISBN 978-0-9522459-1-9

Text © Andrew Bloomfield 2009

Photographs © Gary Smith and Andrew Bloomfield 2009

www.garyksmithphotography.co.uk

Design and layout by Kingfisher Graphics
Email: kingfisher-graphics@sky.com

Printed by Norwich Colour Print Ltd, Drayton, Norwich, UK on Lumi Silk paper using vegetable oil-based inks. The paper, made in Italy, comprises 100% virgin fibre. Pulps used are elemental chlorine-free.

The FSC logo identifies products which contain wood from well-managed forests certified in accordance with the rules of the Forest Stewardship Council.

Contents

Photographs :- All the photographs in this book were taken by Gary Smith, with the exception of pages 13, 14, 21, 23 (top), 26, 34, 36 (bottom), 38 (top right), 39 (top), 42, 43, 45, 51 59, 62 (bottom), 70, 77, 86, 91, 92, 93, 95, 96 (top), 115 and 127 which were taken by Andrew Bloomfield. All the pictures were taken in the wild in North Norfolk, with the exception of the male Bluethroat on page 13 which was taken in Sweden.

Wintering brent geese in Wells Channel.

Preface

The county of Norfolk has many wonderfully conserved natural habitats, each full of their own unique wildlife. Distinct regions such as Breckland, Broadland and the Fens are all rich in natural history but for many people it is the area known as North Norfolk that hosts the most varied collection of flora and fauna and some of the greatest wildlife spectacles in the whole of the county. Despite being a relatively small part of the Norfolk coast, stretching to just over 25 miles between Holme-next-the-Sea in the west and Weybourne in the east, it has long been famed for providing a home to a wide array of species; some often occurring in great abundance. Its affinity with the North Sea is one of the key factors, not only for physically shaping the coast and providing the backdrop to its varied scenery but also in helping to attract many of its birds and animals.

As with any place that has a wide variety of wildlife, the assortment of contrasting environments is the key to North Norfolk's attraction. Sandy beaches, tidal mud flats, salt marshes, fresh water grazing marshes, reed beds, woods, parkland, heaths and intensively farmed arable fields all nestle side by side in the area's mosaic of habitats and each hosts a different selection of inhabitants. Such diversity has resulted in a richness that is seldom matched, let alone bettered, in much of the British Isles and has led to North Norfolk receiving a number of official designations. Area of Outstanding Natural Beauty, Biosphere Reserve, World Heritage Site, North Norfolk Coast Site of Special Scientific Interest (SSSI) and Special Area of Conservation are all accolades that have been bestowed upon significant parts of the region in recognition of local and international importance to nature conservation.

Since the 1970s, the area has changed dramatically: it has become incredibly popular. Holiday developments and the rapid expansion of the tourist infrastructure have seen to that, yet much of the area's character has stemmed from the fact that it was at the hub of a hard working community. In the past most of the population earned a living from either farming or fishing yet it is a sad fact that very few locals are now employed in these industries that made such an impact on both the landscape and the region's heritage. Indeed the impression the area often portrays today is that it is a prosperous playground. Its popularity ensures that much of the coastline is alive with visitors, not only in the summer season, but also increasingly in the winter months. Until comparatively recent times, many of the areas mentioned in this book would be virtually devoid of people in the winter, providing a stark contrast with today's atmosphere.

Nevertheless, North Norfolk has retained much of its identity. Quiet spots and areas of natural beauty can still be found. Its coastline may not be as obviously dramatic as other parts of Britain, but for those with the patience to immerse themselves in the atmosphere of the tidal mud flats and salt marshes, so alive with wildlife and illuminated by a constantly changing sky that stretches unhindered from horizon to horizon and its subtle character will become apparent. Not only must we give credit to the untamed nature of the North Sea for defining the physical geography of the coast but also to the chain of nature reserves that have sprung up along the coast both enhancing and preserving fragile environments. Thanks to past generations of concerned naturalists, nearly every stretch of the coast is owned or managed by a conservation body.

Inland, large estates manage both woods and fields, thus maintaining a suitable habitat for game rearing and the country-shooting scene. Loved and hated amongst the general populace in equal proportions, even conservationists realise that if such practices were to cease then the impetus for retaining such large areas of countryside and home to a wide range of birds and animals could be lost. Although many of today's farming methods have been detrimental to our wildlife, it is also true that the 'great' estates which evolved in the 1700s with innovative agricultural practises shaped much of North Norfolk.

Modern North Norfolk often seems like a place of inharmonious contrast with its rural hamlets, expansive salt marshes and rolling farmland alongside holiday parks with thousands of visitors. Its physical features will continue to change, perhaps beyond all current recognition, due to the predicted global warming, rising sea levels and continued beach erosion, yet its flora and fauna will always adapt to fill whatever niches remain available, ensuring that it remains equally as special to future generations as it has done to those in the past.

Wading birds like these knot, appear in large flocks on North Norfolk's mud flats.

Introduction

The original aim of this book was to create a broad-based appreciation of North Norfolk's natural history, however it soon became apparent that it was becoming rather biased to its birdlife. Most of the area's conservation history is directly linked to birds and the story of the conservation movement's forefathers has become inextricably linked with the North Norfolk we know today, even if a fair proportion of the population do not realise it. Birds and their protection provided the initial reason for conservation bodies to be formed and the county's first reserves to be purchased. Such actions prevented unfavourable developments and have left the area with a coastline that is visited by immense numbers of visitors yet still retains a unique and charming identity.

In the past, the region's reputation was established by the lives of bird collectors and wildfowlers, while at the same time some country estates revolved around the winter sporting scene of shooting game birds. Today, North Norfolk is still nationally famous for the numbers and variety of birds that it attracts although most people now come only to watch them. Indeed the number of people that are drawn to the area by its birds is phenomenal. Recent figures have shown that the RSPB's Titchwell reserve alone welcomes over 86,000 birdwatchers per year. Much of the region's attraction is that at any time of the year there are birds in abundance. Breeding terns and wetland birds in the summer, an assortment of migratory seabirds, waders and passerines in the spring and autumn, enormous flocks of wild geese in the winter, and resident owls and raptors, have all helped to ensure that North Norfolk is very much an all year round destination for the enthusiast.

The distant sand dunes of Blakeney Point as seen from the road into Morston.

So North Norfolk has much to thank for its birdlife. Why then is this book not just about the area's birds? Well, anyone who either lives here or at least is a regular visitor will soon comment on how many other natural splendours there are. Many feel its seals, hares, orchids, butterflies and dragonflies are just as captivating and add to the area's appeal. They are all special enough in their own right, but when combined they paint a far bigger picture; indeed such variety is the very essence of North Norfolk.

This book does not set out to be the last word on North Norfolk's natural history or the ultimate site guide describing every hidden corner. A fully comprehensive textbook this is not, for that would need an encyclopaedic work of several volumes. Instead its aim is to create an appetising taster of what wildlife can be expected in the different habitats, focusing on both the area's characteristic and more unique species. It is hoped that the first time visitor will discover much herein to enthuse over while for those who are familiar with the area, the book should provide information on some of the sights they may encounter and perhaps take for granted.

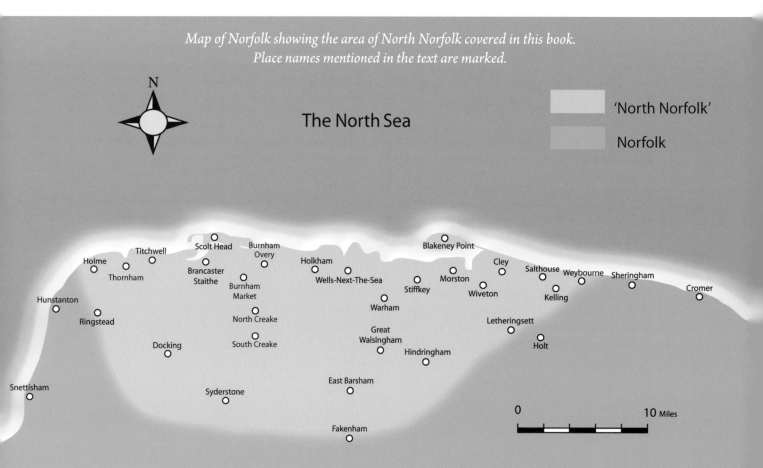

Map of Norfolk showing the area of North Norfolk covered in this book.
Place names mentioned in the text are marked.

Common terns fishing for whitebait in Blakeney Harbour.

Chapter One

A shoreline of terns

The North Sea is the lifeblood of North Norfolk. Its changing moods not only help to create contrasting scenes in the diverse landscape, but directly influence the creatures that appear in it. It has also shaped man's history in the area. Fishing has long been an integral part of the area's economy, with whelks, shrimps, crabs, mussels, cockles and oysters all being gathered at various times throughout history. Sea salt produced at Cley in the 1700s was an important commodity and the network of ports along the coast, formed from humble beginnings in Roman and Saxon times, eventually created great affluence when combined with a growing and thriving agricultural industry within the coast's hinterland.

Not only has the sea directly and indirectly provided an important human heritage, but the coast's wildlife helped to instigate Norfolk's earliest conservationists towards the end of the 1800s and early 1900s. At that time poverty was rife and the majority of Norfolk's rural population took every step available to survive. Wages and living conditions were poor and hard physical labour was the norm. As a result many resorted to the mass exploitation and persecution of local birdlife as a means of supplementing their meagre existence.

Eggs were gathered *en masse*, not only for local food consumption but also to be sold to dealers. The eggs of some species such as black-headed gulls were deemed a delicacy, particularly in London where many ended up. Thousands were gathered in the Blakeney area alone, with dealers paying three old pennies for a dozen eggs in 1834. Such actions proved to be disastrous for several species. Once plentiful birds like lapwings had their eggs collected at

A shelduck with its family.

such a rate that by the 1860s very few nests could be found in their farmland haunts. Not only were the eggs of lapwings treasured but also the birds themselves; their meat being renowned for making splendid pies. One species did actually disappear locally – the avocet. Its eggs were prized for puddings and pancakes while the birds were shot for sport, so much so that by the 1820s breeding had ceased and their appearances were rare.

As species became scarcer, so they became more sought after. Egg collecting in the name of science took the place of pancake production while the fashion of preserving shot birds gathered in pace. The heyday of the gentleman gunners had arrived. These were obsessive wildfowlers and/or collectors of birds; the more unusual the better and North Norfolk's marshes became their favoured haunt. The combined impact of egg and specimen collecting meant that as well as the avocet other species disappeared from Norfolk, such as breeding black-tailed godwits, ruff, marsh harriers and black terns.

It was against this background that the first real conservationists began to make an effort to bring such practises to a halt. A fledgling group, the Norfolk and Norwich Naturalist's Society, was instrumental in highlighting the plight of wild birds and after persistent lobbying, birds and their eggs began to gain far greater protection in a series of Parliamentary Acts. Even more important were the ground breaking steps, taken towards the end of the nineteenth century, to actually create wardened sanctuaries in a closed season where the new laws could be applied. Following the example of Breydon Water near Great Yarmouth two years previously, a local bird protection society was formed at Wells in 1890.

Terns, with their predominantly smart white colouration and black caps, their elegant style of flight and streamlined looks have always been revered by naturalists as being rather special. Both common and little terns were regularly nesting in colonies (or terneries) between Wells and Stiffkey and it was these birds, which benefited from the coast's initial protection efforts. By 1901 a similar scheme had been undertaken in the Blakeney/Cley area, again to preserve dwindling numbers of shore nesting birds such as ringed plovers, oystercatchers and terns. Their eggs also had been regularly gathered by local folk and very few ever produced grown fledglings.

Shelducks, now a familiar sight in our coastline's marshes and harbours, were also suffering wholesale persecution. Dwindling numbers faced the constant barrage of wildfowler's shots in the winter and also persistent egg collecting in the summer. Not only were their eggs taken to eat but also for a far more lucrative market. Clutches were collected from their favoured rabbit burrow nest holes in the dunes and taken to be brooded under domestic ducks. A shelduck was always a welcome addition to a country estate's ornamental lake with landowners often paying the equivalent of a farm workers weekly wage for a mature, wing clipped individual. Artificial rearing of the young ducks, however, was far from easy and many died as a result.

Norfolk's pioneering conservationists then began to look more closely at Blakeney Point. With its shingle foreshore, impressive sand dunes and the vast acreage of adjacent tidal saltings, Blakeney Point was in the 1800's, gaining a fast growing reputation amongst university students, collectors and naturalists alike. From its beginnings at Weybourne to the tip of the far point at Blakeney Harbour almost eight miles away, the specialised flora and fauna of this wave-drenched spit ensured that it gained and maintained such esteemed attention.

Blakeney Point had already gained fame for its breeding terns and it soon became the premier site to search for unusual migrants in the autumn months. Fanatical collectors made the annual pilgrimage to scour the limited coastal vegetation in the hope of shooting any rarity. The large arrivals of migrant songbirds from northern Europe, displaced by east or northeast winds over the North Sea whilst travelling south to their wintering grounds in Africa, became an eagerly anticipated phenomenon. Most prized and sought after were bluethroats. These robin-like birds with vivid red, blue and white face and throat markings breed in the dwarf willow thickets of Scandinavian bogs and highlands and these days appear rarely (only two or

Bluethroats were a regular autumn quarry species in the 1800s. Today they are very rare.

Norfolk's first desert wheatear was obtained at Blakeney Point in 1907.
This male was at Holkham in November 1999.

three per year in the whole of Norfolk). In the 1800s, however, they were more plentiful. September 1884 must have been something special indeed compared with today's standards, as 80-100 were supposedly present in the Blakeney/Cley area alone. Grey, murky mornings with onshore winds consequently became known as "bluethroat mornings" and amongst the vast quantities of common birds such as redstarts and robins, which were often shot and discarded by the bucket full, came the rarities. Yellow-breasted bunting and Pallas's warbler from the taiga forests of Siberia were new to Britain, while little bunting and yellow-browed warbler (also from Siberia) and desert wheatear from the deserts of the Middle East and North Africa, were all new additions to Norfolk's bird list.

Thanks to the already proven success of wardening nesting shore birds, the National Trust felt the opportunity of purchasing Blakeney Point too great to miss and in 1912 it became Norfolk's first fully protected nature reserve. With an area of about 539 hectares eventually purchased more progress was soon occurring. Once the locals had begrudgingly become accustomed to the idea of nature preservation, Blakeney Point's breeding birds began to thrive again. When seasonal wardening had commenced in 1901, 140 pairs of common terns and 60 pairs of little terns were nesting, with little success. Shelduck were hanging on in small numbers while oystercatchers, which had been described as abundant breeders in the early 1800s, had disappeared completely from Cley and Blakeney by 1892. A single pair returned in 1906 with a steady increase thereafter. Little tern numbers increased to 100 pairs by 1912 while common terns positively thrived, reaching 500 pairs in the 1920s and an impressive 2000 pairs between 1935 and 1940.

Above: Sandwich terns first produced young at Blakeney Point in 1920.

Below: The common tern nests along the shoreline often perilously close to the tideline.

Another species of tern became synonymous with the Point – the sandwich tern. Today it is one of coastal Norfolk's most conspicuous sea birds and also a harbinger of Spring, arriving in the first wave of migrants in mid March. It may therefore be surprising to know it was unrecorded locally until 1891 when one was shot at Cley/Blakeney. The first breeding report followed a few years later when two pairs nested although their finders promptly cooked and ate the eggs! Thankfully appearances of sandwich terns increased and a pair that joined the common tern colony in 1920, nested with successful results. Numbers swiftly built up to nine nests in 1922, 100 in 1923 and 1500 in 1929.

Also found nesting on the Point was the arctic tern. Somewhat similar in appearance to a common tern it sports even longer tail streamers, whiter more translucent wings and a thicker blood red bill. Ongoing studies from caught and ringed terns have shown that common terns overwinter around much of the African continent (although like sandwich terns they favour the west coast) in contrast to arctic terns which undertake even lengthier migrations. In fact the distances involved make the arctic terns' movements between breeding and wintering grounds the most extensive of any bird. With a nesting range that takes in the far north of Greenland, Iceland and much of northern Canada and northern Europe they then migrate south into the southern hemisphere as far as the Antarctic and Australia. With Norfolk being further south than much of their British breeding range, the first nest at Blakeney in 1922 was very welcome. The following year saw ten pairs breed. Annual nesting was noted thereafter with an eventual peak of 20 pairs in more modern times between 1993 and 1998.

Arctic terns first nested at Blakeney Point in 1922. Small numbers still breed today.

Scolt Head Island is one of the least disturbed areas along the North Norfolk coast.

With the purchase of Blakeney Point proving to be such a huge success, local conservationists were not long in drawing up their plans for another similar acquisition, the island of Scolt Head. Taking in almost four miles of the coastline between the harbours of Burnham Overy and Brancaster it is remote, weather beaten and one of North Norfolk's quietest areas. Its habitats include tidal mud flats and creeks, low lying salt marshes, sand and shingle foreshore and old established dunes, one of which is the highest in Norfolk. Like much of North Norfolk's coast, Scolt Head has ancient roots and is still evolving; changing in shape and structure thanks to the constant building up of beach sediments and subsequent erosive battering it receives from winds and strong tidal currents.

Scolt Head has much in common with Blakeney Point. It has a similar physical geography, coastal flora and breeding birds, yet it differs in the fact that it is an island cut off from the mainland by tidal creeks and channels. This remoteness and inaccessibility has undoubtedly added to its charm and also contributed to it attracting equally as important numbers of breeding terns as Blakeney Point. The two sites had always been held in equal esteem and many conservationists felt to safeguard both would be a beneficial move and this is what happened in 1923.

Like Blakeney Point, Scolt Head soon reaped the benefits of protection. When wardening commenced in 1922, common terns only numbered 17 pairs but by 1925 had increased to 700-1000 pairs and a record 2470 by 1938. Little terns increased to 100 pairs by 1927 and 200 pairs in 1937. Sandwich terns became an annual breeder following the first nest in 1923 and by 1946 up to 1900 pairs were present. North Norfolk's other two scarcer terns; the roseate and arctic also nested in small numbers commencing in 1903 and 1938 respectively. Oystercatchers increased noticeably from seven pairs in 1924 to an impressive 92 by 1947. Ringed plovers too grew in number with 67 pairs in 1924 increasing to an unbelievable 250 by 1957. Scolt Head, like Blakeney Point gained a worthy reputation for being one of Europe's most important sites for breeding shore birds, terns in particular.

Blakeney Point is still as popular today as it was in the past although the visitors now arrive to appreciate its wildlife rather more humanely. Its popularity is boosted further in the summer by day tripping tourists and over 50,000 visitors per year are now expected at Blakeney Point, making the roping off of tern colonies and regular wardening even more essential. With regular ferries serving the tip of the Point at high water, the four mile trek from Cley can be bypassed and when combined with a trip to see the harbour's seal population, it could be argued that there is no finer place along the coast for experiencing the wildlife of North Norfolk. Furthermore by visiting a place like Blakeney Point, which is very much prepared for large numbers of visitors, other more vulnerable areas can be left undisturbed.

The sandwich tern is these days the most abundant of North Norfolk's breeding seabirds. It is impossible to walk along the beaches in mid summer and not see an almost constant procession passing to and fro along the shore, many carrying sand eels in their bills. Breeding colonies, however, still remain the place to gain a more intimate view during the six months that they spend in Britain.

The sandwich tern breeding colony at Blakeney Point.

They nest in tightly packed colonies on remote and isolated shingle ridges beyond the reach of the tide. Nesting amidst black-headed gull colonies is also a preference, as in the early stages of breeding it is these noisy, aggressive birds that are the first to rise and see off anything seeming to pose a threat. For sandwich terns, a disturbance free environment is essential as they are quick to desert if frequently harassed during their preliminary days of courtship and incubation. With Scolt and Blakeney both suitable sites, numbers vary from year to year with either one or the other attracting the majority of the population. Numbers peaked at a combined total of 5600 pairs in 1979, with 4800 pairs at Scolt in 1972 being the largest colony count.

Tern colonies are probably most captivating early in the season when the pairs are busy courting or in late June when the parents are constantly bringing in fish to feed their offspring. An early spring visit on one of the boat trips to Blakeney Point is as good an introduction as any to watch terns. The air is filled with the clamour of the shrieking birds and on closer inspection, their enchanting courtship ceremonies can be witnessed with ease. Each tern species has a similar ritual in which the male presents his mate with a fish. It forms part of regular pair bonding and often precedes copulation. The sandwich tern's actions are arguably the most spectacular, due in part to the dense colonies which they form and that all around pairs will be undertaking the same behaviour. Males arrive, each grasping a fish, whereupon they stand proud, with neck and head held high and crests often erect. As they stretch up, their wings are pressed forward and downwards. This characteristic pose is then maintained as the pair struts around, until the female finally accepts the fish. Both birds then hold their heads even higher, followed by a bout of head turning. In the early stages of courtship, males often hold onto the fish and fly off high into the sky, constantly calling and followed by one or more persistently begging females. These activities are only a glimpse into the daily routine of nesting terns and for those with dedication, their behaviour, be it courtship, feeding or parenting their young, makes fascinating viewing.

The other most frequently seen species is the common tern, although numbers fail to reach the impressive levels of the 1930s and 1940s. The status of little and arctic terns remains similar to the past. Common and little terns nest in smaller more scattered colonies than sandwich terns preferring sandy beaches where shingle and pebbles render their cryptic eggs almost invisible to the untrained eye. In contrast to Scolt's record 2470 pairs of common terns in 1938, recent years have seen a decline to 600 pairs in the 1970s and 300 pairs in 2000 being the best modern total. The same can be said at Blakeney where a maximum of 1800 pairs in the 1960s had dwindled to 168 pairs by 2003. Little terns have in recent years managed to reach a high of 160 pairs at Scolt in 2008 and 215 pairs at Blakeney in 1996.

Tern numbers fluctuate all along the coast, with threats from human disturbance, bad weather, high tides and natural predation from kestrels, foxes, rats, stoats and common, herring and lesser black-backed gulls all combining to produce the occasional poor breeding season. Illegal egg collecting by selfish individuals, whilst not to the scale of Victorian times, still manages to pose a threat. In the case of both common and particularly little terns their quest

The little tern is one of the UK's scarcest breeding seabirds.

for success is often hampered by the fact that their nest sites are often not quite far enough away from the high water mark during the largest of tides. At Scolt Head, wardens have successfully resorted to giving vulnerable nests a bit of extra height by moving them into old washing up bowls on top of upturned buckets to prevent nest flooding. Chick mortality and nest desertion or destruction is often caused by freak summer storms, high tides, wind blown sand and salt-water foam. Nevertheless a few other localities along the coast also provide attractive nesting sites and there is always an alternative for this delightful family of birds, ensuring that North Norfolk is still very much the shoreline of terns that those early conservationists had hoped for.

Although breeding terns are the most prized inhabitants of the shoreline there are several other species that also benefit from protection. Most conspicuous are shelducks and oystercatchers particularly when undertaking their lengthy, noisy bouts of courtship and territorial disputes in the spring. Small groups of shelducks are a common sight on warm April days, searching out suitable rabbit burrows in which to nest. Their braying laugh-like calls are frequently heard especially when disturbed, but the male's vigorous head flicking and neck stretching display, which often climaxes with aggressive confrontations with his rivals needs more patience to observe.

The oystercatcher's bold displays, however, include calls so loud that they are one of the coast's most familiar and far-reaching sounds. Their shrill vocalisations reach fever pitch as the birds rush about on the ground, with hunched back, head held forward and bill angled downwards. Oystercatchers nest on the sand blown dunes almost as frequently as they do on the foreshore's higher shingle ridges. Here, along with the terns, the ringed plover is still to be found nesting. Long associated with the North Norfolk coast, its confiding manner makes it quite a well-known and easily recognisable bird. The number of old local names such as 'stonerunner', 'sand dotterel', 'ringed dotterel' and 'stonehatch' bears testament to that.

An increasingly scarce sight on many North Norfolk beaches is a nesting ringed plover.

An unusual oystercatcher nest site; a dead tree at Thornham.

Not as noisy as oystercatchers, male ringed plovers still manage to put on quite an elaborate display ritual on warm days in March and April when they set about claiming a territory and a mate. Slow flapping and gliding song flights usually end with frantic chases on the ground, with the males running around, bodies bent forward, tails held upwards and spread out like a fan. With some undisturbed beaches attracting a pair every 20 metres or so, skirmishes between neighbouring males can frequently be observed.

While we have seen that both ringed plovers and oystercatchers increased after the concerted efforts of the early conservationists, modern times have seen changing fortunes for the two species. Oystercatcher numbers have continued to grow, averaging at 390 pairs along the coast per year since 1995, with 200 nests at Blakeney Point in 1998 being the maximum from a single site. These days oystercatchers are not, however, solely a coastal bird with many now breeding on adjacent grazing marshes and inland on arable fields.

Ringed plovers, however, have not fared quite so well. They have averaged at about 160 pairs along the coast since 1995, from which Blakeney Point's population has dropped from a high of 75 pairs in 1996 to as low as 12 pairs in 2006. Scolt Head, still very much the last remaining 'wilderness' of North Norfolk in regards to low visitor numbers, remains the species stronghold. Numbers surpassing 100 pairs have not been reached here since 1988, although the site still managed to attract 79 pairs in 2007. Sparrowhawks have frequently been seen taking adult plovers off the beaches and natural predation is just as problematic as disturbance from holidaymakers. On popular beaches nesting shore birds face a regular passage of passers-by, often resulting in incubating parents constantly having to leave their eggs thus leaving them more exposed to predators. While many of the larger more obvious colonies of shore birds benefit from being roped off, there are still just as many isolated pairs which either desert completely or face high chick mortality such is the pressure from modern day recreation. It is hoped that the ringed plover's fortunes can be reversed with the provision of wire mesh cages which conservation workers have begun to place over nest scrapes since 2004. This at least gives the eggs protection from voracious avian predators like the common gull.

If the plovers can manage to hatch their eggs then the sight of tiny, long legged and dappled earthy brown chicks brooding tight under their mother can be seen along the coast from mid May to July. Get too close, however, and the female will soon run off, twisting and tumbling with one wing held out as if broken; a distraction display aimed solely at taking the attention away from her precious offspring. Unlike the ringed plover chicks that are quite cable of feeding themselves on tiny insects soon after birth, the oystercatcher's young need constant attention and their parents constantly fly back and forth with food for their young. Marine invertebrates such as worms and cockles are favoured food items, yet, when nesting amongst other coastal birds, occasional rogue oystercatchers have been known to smash eggs or even kill the small chicks of nearby nesting terns.

Whereas oystercatchers and ringed plovers patiently rear offspring on the dunes and beaches close to their nest sites, shelducks undertake very different behaviour. Their broods of tiny pied ducklings sometimes numbering as many as 15, are very vulnerable out on the open dunes and need water to aid their protection. Soon after birth at the end of May or early June, the young will be marched off towards salt marsh creeks or freshwater pools. Distances travelled can sometimes be a few miles, as some birds nest inland in straw stacks, undisturbed farm buildings or hollow trees.

Migrant songbirds are still just as actively searched for, although these days it is obsessive birdwatchers that are scouring the bushes for them as opposed to shooters and collectors. Numbers of migrants are undoubtedly less compared to the past yet this does little to dampen the spirits of the dedicated birder in search of the unusual. Onshore winds with rain or mist still offer the opportunity for a 'fall' and amidst the commoner species such as wheatears, redstarts, whinchats, pied flycatchers and willow warblers in the early autumn there will be the chance of finding scarcer species such as red-backed shrikes, wrynecks, barred, greenish and icterine warblers. There are other coastal sites watched just as avidly as the Point; realistically anywhere that provides cover for temporarily grounded migrants can be worthwhile although Holme, Scolt Head, Overy Dunes and the Holkham/Wells area consistently attract something of great interest. Amongst the common and the scarce there is always the likelihood of finding something exceptional. Birds from different points around Europe such as pied, black-eared

Above: The pied flycatcher is most frequent during north east winds in August and September.

Below: Some migrants travel immense distances such as this yellow-browed warbler from Siberia.

February 27th is the earliest date for a returning wheatear in the spring.

and isabelline wheatears, lesser grey shrikes, hoopoes, ortolan and rustic buntings, arctic, subalpine, Sardinian and Ruppell's warblers are just some exciting examples of north coast rarities from recent years.

In the past the collectors' efforts were aimed solely at August and September but today with the realisation that the autumn migration actually continues until November the variety of birds seen has become even greater. In late autumn when migrant song thrushes, blackbirds, redwings, fieldfares, robins and goldcrests can abound there is always the chance of finding scarce northern birds such as great grey shrikes, long-eared owls, waxwings and mealy redpolls while the chance of a lost Siberian vagrant becomes even more possible, particularly if high pressure systems and easterly winds stretch across Europe.

The tiny, brightly coloured Pallas's and yellow-browed warblers that undertake such a seemingly impossible journey for species so small are now regular, with some years providing bumper numbers. The wooded dunes at Holkham and Wells offer the best opportunity and single day totals of Pallas's warblers reached ten (on October 15th 1982) and yellow-browed warblers 18 (on October 12th 1988). For species that had not been recorded prior to the late 1800s it seems hard to believe that between 1963 and 2008 there have been at least 78 Pallas's warblers and 418 yellow-browed warblers recorded from this one locality. To witness a party of newly arrived goldcrests flitting amidst the golden yellow foliage of an autumn sycamore tree and suddenly come across one of these brightly marked Asian warblers is without doubt one of the highlights of autumn birdwatching on the coast.

A long list of even more extreme Asian rarities have been found over the years in North Norfolk with some such as dusky and Radde's warblers, olive-backed pipit, desert wheatear, little bunting and isabelline shrike providing more records than birds like black-throated and siberian thrushes, red-flanked bluetail, yellow-browed bunting, two-barred greenish, paddyfield, Blyth's reed, Hume's and Pallas's grasshopper warblers that have only appeared infrequently or even on single occasions. There is no denying, however, that the most unlikely of North Norfolk's long list of passerine vagrants come from North America.

A diminutive red-breasted nuthatch arrived at Holkham in October 1989 to remain for the winter and to date remains the sole British record. Similarly a white-crowned sparrow remained at Cley between January and March in 2008. It had only been seen on five previous occasions before in Britain and attracted so many admirers during its stay that donations close to £6500 were raised to fund church restorations.

Above: The wryneck is a scarce migrant from Scandinavia seen in the spring and autumn.

Below: Newly arrived redwings seeking a welcome drink after a long migration.

Above: Fieldfares from northern Europe feasting on sea buckthorn berries at Holme.

Left: Migrant birds still arrive during the winter, the waxwing being the most eagerly anticipated.

Below: This white-crowned sparrow from North America wintered at Cley in 2008.

Grey seals with their young at Blakeney Point.

Chapter Two

Seals and sand dunes

Many first time visitors to North Norfolk make their initial forays into exploring the coast and its wildlife by taking one of the regular boat trips from Morston to visit Blakeney Point's seal colony. The experience has become so popular that it has often been voted the most popular 'natural' tourist attraction in the county.

The desolate tip of the Point with its virtually inaccessible sand bars at the harbour's mouth provides the ideal location for the seals to gather. Despite the regular visits, they seem to take little notice of boats full of noisy people. They are close to rich feeding waters and convenient for an easy escape into deep water if danger threatens. Although small numbers of seals can be observed dotted anywhere along the offshore waters there is certainly no substitute for seeing them hauled out on Blakeney's tidal sands.

Two species of seal are actually present at Blakeney; common seals and grey seals. The common seal is the world's most widely distributed species of seal, inhabiting the shores of western and northern Europe, southern Greenland, most of North America and across the Pacific to the coasts of Siberia and Japan. In Britain it is found in its greatest numbers around Scotland while scattered groups down England's east coast reach their peak around the Wash. Close monitoring has revealed that seals frequently move between the Wash and Blakeney, while some have travelled northwards to Scotland and across the North Sea to haul-out sites along the coasts of Holland and France.

Grey seals are on average much larger creatures than commons; the bulls in particular have been recorded up to 72 stone (450 kgs) in weight and 7 feet (2.20 metres) in length, making them other than whales, Britain's largest regularly occurring mammals. Both species produce their young on the Point. The pups differ markedly not only in looks but also in some of their biological traits. In contrast to the common's summer birth period, greys produce their pups between October and December. Grey seals are born bearing a beautiful white coat, which moults to grey after three weeks. They are also completely dependent on their mother for protection as they are unable to swim and mortality is often heightened by careless observers, whose presence at close quarters is sometimes enough to drive the mother away from her pup. During the breeding season the female builds up an extra thick layer of blubber prior to birthing, giving her a rotund, bloated appearance and for three to four weeks she does not feed herself, surviving solely from her own fat reserves. Such is the richness of her milk, the pup will treble its body weight in three to four weeks after which time it is left to fend for itself. The females are by then not only much thinner but also at the height of fertility and will mate with a dominant bull. He will have staked his supremacy after a number of what can be vicious clashes, with rival males.

Young common seals, in contrast to greys, can swim an hour or two after birth and most have shed their white pre-natal coat while still in their mother's womb giving them a very different appearance. The fact that common seal pups are able to take to the water when so young has perhaps helped the species become more successful and widespread and not so reliant upon remote, safe breeding sites as grey seals.

A courting pair of grey seals on the shoreline at Blakeney.

Grey seals have only recently become established here whereas common seals have long been a resident of our coast. Their popularity, however, is a far more recent phenomenon as in the past they were often despised by fishermen and exploited as much as birds were. Even some early conservationists cared little for seals with Robert Pinchen, an early warden of Blakeney Point, pronouncing that "their presence was not required", despite frequently seeing up to 50 around the harbour in the 1920s. Seals' thick pelts were once greatly valued by the clothing industry, with shoes and saddle covers being other popular end products. There is even an old report from the early 1900s at Blakeney where a 16 stone bull seal was killed for its pelt to produce the back of a lady's coat. A further eight pelts from smaller seals were also required to complete it. The thick layer of blubber was also highly sought after, as when refined, the resulting oil could be used to fuel lamps and also feed livestock in the winter months.

Another fascinating tale from the Eastern Daily Press in 1911, describes how the Eastern Fisheries Board thought that the culling of all 200 of the Wash's seals would be most beneficial to the fishermen of the area. Indeed at Hunstanton in the 1920s, seal hunting on the offshore sandbars was actually advertised in a tourist guide under a heading 'things to do'. Such talk and speculation as to the potential damage caused by seals to fish stocks continued through much of the twentieth century and indeed at Blakeney in the 1930s, the Ministry of Fisheries paid ten shillings for every shot seal's nose they received. This finally came to an end when stomach content analysis of dead seals proved that instead of flat fish it was whelks, crabs and other shellfish, which were in fact the favoured diet of Blakeney's seals.

Elsewhere, however, the slaughter continued and actually increased in many places. By the 1950s and 1960s seals were being culled in large numbers in the Wash. Particularly valued were the coats of pups. Images in the local press of defenceless seal pups getting clubbed to death combined with the growing numbers of shot seals (some still alive) being washed up onto local beaches helped turn public opinion very much against the seal hunters. Figures from the Wash revealed that as many as 5000 seals were killed between 1962 and 1970 of which 800 pups were shot in 1969 alone! The Wash population had been estimated at 2000-4000 in 1962 with a further 100-300 regularly at Blakeney throughout the 1960s and it was obvious that unless such slaughter was halted a very grim future may have been ahead for the seals. Mounting pressure finally resulted in the 1970 Conservation of Seals Act that created a closed season for breeding seals and finally a complete ban on culling came in 1974.

With the slaughter brought to an end, a bright future seemed guaranteed and indeed for a while they thrived. Blakeney's herd reached 220 in 1972 and 750 by the mid 1980s. Unfortunately success was short lived as another potentially more disastrous setback arose in 1988 when an outbreak of a fatal contagious disease known as Phocine Distemper Virus (or PDV) emerged, killing 1500 of Norfolk's common seals in the process. Prior to striking Britain's east coast, the virus had already caused havoc in Europe, where up to 18,000 common seals died. As for its origins, some scientists suggested it was brought into western Europe by the harp seal, a species usually at home in the Arctic Ocean around Northern Russia, Greenland, Spitsbergen and eastern Canada. Unusually high numbers of this cream bodied seal, with distinctive dark face and back, appeared in the northern waters of the North Sea in 1988. Thousands were trapped in fishing nets off Norway and one even managed to find its way to Blakeney Harbour, where it was found freshly dead on March 27th (the only other local record is of one found at Holkham and taken into care in 1994).

Whatever caused the virus, it certainly had a major impact and Norfolk lost as much as 60% of its common seal population. Numbers at Blakeney were slow to recover with counts of 100 in October 1990, 300 in 1993 and 330 in 1995 being less than half their previous high in the mid 1980s. With such an uphill struggle occurring, the news in 2002 of another outbreak was even

Common seals hauled out alongside Blakeney Channel.

more devastating. By October, 4000 had died in Scandinavia and over 1000 here on England's east coast. Over 200 were washed up dead over a three-month period at Holkham Bay and 120 between Cley and Stiffkey. Since then the Blakeney population once more recovered, reaching 530 by August 2006.

Whereas the virus hit common seals hard, the grey seal remained largely unaffected. Grey seals are more associated with rocky coastlines and uninhabited islands with their world range encompassing the east coast of North America, Iceland, the Faeroes, Norway, North West Russia, the Baltic Sea and in Britain. Here they are most abundant along the Scottish coast, also inhabiting western Ireland, Wales, southwest England and down the east coast. The Farne Isles provide a home for a large population and monitoring has shown that many of Norfolk's grey seals originated there. Despite first being noted in the county as recently as 1881, when two were killed near King's Lynn, followed by North Norfolk's first at Wells in 1892, grey seals did not become firmly established until much later. The first breeding in North Norfolk occurred at Scolt Head between 1951 and 1953 and they started to appear off Blakeney by the mid 1960s with a few finally becoming resident by 1979. By the late 1980s the first breeding attempts at Blakeney were noted. In 1993 up to 50 were counted, doubling to over 100 in 1994. Numbers peak during the autumn at the height of the breeding season. When numbers are high further north, dominant bulls will drive off less powerful or younger males, which consequently journey south to find their own harem of females to mate with. With a substantial population regularly off the Lincolnshire coast at Donna Nook and breeding now noted annually in east Norfolk at Horsey, the grey seal is a species which could well increase still further, both at Blakeney and perhaps on other remote spots along our coastline. Indeed in 2008 up to 700 adults and an unprecedented 400 pups were counted on the end of the Point.

Apart from common and grey, there have been the occasional records of lost vagrant species of seals in North Norfolk, such as the harp seal previously mentioned. One of the most interesting records is a bearded seal, noted for the first time in British waters at Burnham Overy in February 1892. It must have been quite weak or tame as it was caught and exhibited at various places around the country. Perhaps understandably it eventually died, although its skull was put on display in the University Museum of Zoology at Cambridge. The unfortunate beast was far away from its normal range in the pack ice and polar seas to the north of Scandinavia, Iceland and Greenland and has yet to be recorded in Norfolk again. The bearded seal is a large species sometimes measuring up to 12 feet in length, plain brown/grey in colour and has long curled whiskers. An even larger species is the hooded seal, the adult male of which displays a large fleshy proboscis from which it inflates a peculiar round membrane when courting on its breeding grounds in the arctic pack ice. In recent years small but increasing numbers of stranded juveniles have been found on the English east coast, including singles at Holkham in August 1996 and October 2006. A far smaller arctic species, the ringed seal, has also been found once (also a lost juvenile) on the beach at Wells in July 1995.

While seals and terns are arguably amongst the premier attractions of North Norfolk's coast in the summer months, there is another equally important selection of flora and fauna, which help to make the shoreline such a distinctive habitat. Its tidal sands, wind swept dunes and sea drenched shingle ridges often appear empty and perhaps barren to those who only give them a cursory glance, but they do in fact harbour a rich variety of plants and insects which rely on such places to exist and in some cases are found nowhere else in the area.

The yellow-horned poppy is common on the shingle between Weybourne and Blakeney.

The coastline is an ever-changing environment. Unpredictable weather and sea conditions can rapidly change physical features and some of our plant communities exist in a fragile, sometimes temporary world. Species such as marram and sand couch grass are most important to coastal stability, binding the sand together and forming fledgling dune systems but as the maturing process accelerates, so does the diversity of plants, producing even more colour and charm to the coastline.

One of the most unappealing places for plants might initially appear to be the desolate and exposed shingle spit between Weybourne and Blakeney. But even here some quite remarkable plants flourish. They exist above the mean high water mark, usually on the landward side in sometimes very dry conditions, surviving thanks to moisture produced from heavy dews, and humus from organic tidal debris. Among the larger and more conspicuous plants is the yellow horned poppy. Apart from its yellow flowers it also differs from a field poppy with its paler grey-green, crinkled more papery leaves and its exceptionally long horn-like seedpods that sometimes reach 12 inches in length. Its distinctive leaves are specially adapted to reduce water loss, a feature shared by other plants that inhabit the shoreline.

Less showy, but equally attractive is sea campion, another exclusively maritime plant, with a white flower head, which positively thrives at Blakeney and Cley. It grows in dense low-lying mats often close to patches of the small and succulent sea sandwort, another plant, which, like marram grass, is a colonist of new sand dune ridges. Shrubby sea blite (frequently referred to by its botanical name *suaeda*) is a dense, woody bush that grows in obvious belts alongside creeks or close to the high water mark of salt marshes. This nationally scarce species is most characteristic of North Norfolk's coastline. It too finds the shingle bank at Blakeney a suitable area on which to grow. Here it is particularly famed amongst bird watchers who search through it religiously throughout the autumn months for newly arrived migrant songbirds. With limited vegetation available in which to feed and shelter, the plentiful stands of this thick shrub act as the perfect temporary refuge. At other times of the year it also provides the perfect site for nesting reed buntings, dunnocks and wrens in an area with very few other alternatives.

Sea thrift or as it is sometimes known, sea pink, seems just as at home on the shingle ridge as it does on the sea cliffs of northern Britain. Its elegant pink flowers are a common sight in May and June. Another specialised shingle loving plant, sea kale with its mass of large crinkled blue-green leaves and its crown of small tightly packed white flowers, was in the 1800s described as abundant along much of North Norfolk's coast but it dwindled to become a scarcity. It now only remains at one site; Blakeney Point where it was reintroduced in 1912. In years gone by, the plant's newly emerging shoots were deemed edible delicacies, although its disappearance from many British sites has been blamed upon coastal erosion and at Cley on the continual bulldozing up of the shingle bank to reinforce coastal stability. Now that the Environment Agency have deemed this an unviable piece of coastal protection work it will be interesting to see what the future holds for the whole of this fragile shingle beach and how the remaining species of flora are affected.

Moving further west, the shingle spit of Blakeney merges with sand blown ridges and embryo dunes, a habitat that is in fact plentiful along the whole coast. Still faced with a frequent pounding from wind and sea it would perhaps seem just as uninviting for plants yet more species find their niche here and like the marram and sand couch grasses, help further to stabilise the shifting sands. Where the tide line meets the dunes, large clumps of pink flowered, rubbery stemmed sea rocket, dense tangles of prickly saltwort, whose green fleshy leaves end with sharp spines, and the frosted orache (a frail looking plant with silver green curled leaves) sometimes grow in such abundance it seems as if they are acting as a final barrier for the waves which frequently lap around their stems. One species, which is more numerous in the young

A grayling butterfly visiting the flowers of sea holly.

outer dunes from Holkham through to Scolt Head, is sea holly. As its name suggests its prickly leaves resemble those of the common holly of our hedgerows, but this is as far as the comparison goes. Instead of reaching tall bush proportions and sporting a crop of red berries in the autumn, sea holly is a low growing plant with leaves that have a very pale frosted colouration while its subtle lilac blue flowers appear in July and August. Another plant commonly encountered on Scolt Head in the newer dunes is the sea spurge, a succulent perennial whose multitude of short leaves sprout forth and overlap each other up the length of the stem, culminating in a cluster of insignificant tight green flower heads. If broken, a distinctive milky, white liquid oozes out of its stem.

With age, the freshly blown sand of the unstable pioneering dunes is replaced by a far more permanent base of mosses, lichens and grasses. Here a wide array of flora is able to establish itself, creating a far different appearance to the sands immediately adjacent to the shore. Amidst the shallow turf there are a number of localised specialities some peculiar to the coast, others not, but when combined, the visual effect of the annual blaze of colour can be quite stunning.

One of the finest and most accessible spots for enjoying typical dune flora is the one-mile stretch from the western end of Holkham pine woods to the mouth of Burnham Overy Harbour. In June in the damper low lying areas of dunes, deep pink southern marsh and the common spotted orchids (their dark blotched leaves giving them their name) are found, sometimes in quite dense clumps. Having gone to seed in July, they are replaced by more dainty, yellow white flowered marsh helleborines, common here but very much a localised species on the coast in general. The dunes at Holme are an equally important site with swathes of the latter growing alongside the even more localised early marsh orchid. Here this is found as the form *coccinea*, a beautiful red subspecies that is found in few other spots in the county *(see picture on page 2)*.

The most instantly recognisable and arguably most impressive orchid is the bee orchid which can appear in good numbers at Overy. It is so named because its flower head resembles a bumble bee. Bee orchids are usually at their best in mid June after which they are replaced by pyramidal orchids, another distinctive species that grows in even larger numbers. They are so named due to the newly emerging flower heads pyramidal shape. Perched on slender stems, their quaint blooms vary from pale pinks to stronger violets. Every year a group of pure white flowers appear but they are in a rare minority. While bee orchids have long since given up their evolutionary habit of relying on bees for pollination (being easily self pollinated), pyramidal orchids have evolved to survive solely with the help of certain insects. Their pollen is located in such a position that only the proboscis of a butterfly or moth can reach it. This phenomenon can often be seen on sunny days when meadow browns, dark green fritillaries and burnet moths constantly jostle each other to gain poll position on a favoured flower head.

Sea bindweed is another widely distributed plant. It has long creeping stems and sports large pale pink and yellow bell like flowers and it grows profusely amongst North Norfolk's older dunes. While some of North Norfolk's plants are unique to the coast, others are even more important as they are rare at a national level. The end of Blakeney Point hosts the delicate feathery tussocks of grey hair grass. Here it is far from scarce, but nationally it remains a rarity. Even more unusual is the Jersey cudweed, a rather small, insignificant, slender stemmed August flowering plant. By 1918 it had disappeared from all of its former Breckland haunts and for much of the twentieth century was only known to exist in one mainland site in Britain; the dunes slacks at Burnham Overy.

Southern marsh orchids and bird's foot trefoil growing in profusion at Burnham Overy.

The bee orchid's name came from the flowers resemblance to a bumble bee.

The man orchid is a rarity on the North Norfolk coast.

Below: The white form of pyramidal orchid remains very scarce.

Marsh helleborines are abundant at Holme, Holkham and Wells.

Another rarity that grows at one protected site along the coast (and is the sole Norfolk locality) is the man orchid. It was discovered here as recently as 1981. Rather more impressive than Jersey cudweed or grey hair grass, it is an early June flowering plant. Each flower in its dainty clusters has a vague resemblance to a human body; complete with head, arms and legs. Man orchids are primarily found on chalk and limestone grassland in southern England, albeit locally and in decline, and their isolated outpost amongst Norfolk's dunes is also far from flourishing.

As there is such an array of colour produced by the variety of wild flowers, it is not surprising that a varied selection of insect life also flourishes in the area's dunes. Most conspicuous are butterflies. The tiny, powder-blue coloured common blue flies abundantly over the dunes in May/June and again during a second hatching in August/September. Other species such as the small copper, small heath and meadow brown are also common. In contrast, the grayling, brown argus and dark green fritillary are much more localised. Graylings are on the wing from July into September, but their frequent habit of landing with wings held tightly closed, combined with their cryptic colouration sometimes makes them very difficult to see.

The same could not be said of the dark green fritillary. This large butterfly with black chequered, orange upper wings and silver spotted and green toned under wings, is a startling sight as it darts about amongst the flower heads of thistles, pyramidal orchids, sea holly and privet in the dunes at Scolt Head and Burnham Overy. The first warm days in late June trigger an emergence, with July seeing a peak in both activity and numbers. Their eggs are laid low to the ground on violets, the favoured food plant of their caterpillars.

While the dark green fritillary is one of the larger butterflies likely to be encountered, the brown argus is one of the smallest. They are immaculate little insects; their dark brown upper wings adorned with small orange spots and a white trim around their rear edges. Despite expanding over much of the county since the 1980s they are found at some of their highest densities along our coastline.

Two six-spotted burnet moths on a pyramidal orchid.   *Sea bindweed is a common plant on the coastal dunes.*

The painted lady is a migrant species that arrives here from Europe and North Africa. It appears annually, sometimes in great numbers, as it did in June 1996, 2003 and again in late May 2009. This last year was one of the biggest ever arrivals witnessed, as wave after wave appeared sometimes pausing only briefly before moving west. On May 24th alone over 1000 per hour passed along the coast with many others inland too. Another migrant insect that can be very abundant is the silver-y moth and it carries out its search for nectar in daylight. This allows the tiny pale 'Y' markings on its mottled grey upper wings, which gives it its name, to be seen.

Even more distinctive is the hummingbird hawk-moth. With its long proboscis and its darting, hovering flight it is sometimes mistaken as a hummingbird. It appears annually particularly during hot weather. Whilst plants such as valerian readily attract them inland, on the dunes, bedstraw is often visited. Scarcer and equally spectacular species also appear. The broad-bordered bee hawk-moth is very similar to the hummingbird hawk but looks more like a bumble bee and it too can be seen feeding in daylight, hovering around the flower heads of pink campion at Holkham in May and June. Another lover of these flowers is the Bedstraw hawk-moth, a large and brightly coloured migrant species that occasionally appears in the early summer months. Although it remains a national rarity, other more common relatives seen in the wooded dunes at Holkham include the elephant hawk-moth with its bright pink colouration, the emperor moth with its 'eye' like wing markings and the large privet hawk-moth to name but a few of the more striking species. One moth that is much easier to see is the six-spotted burnet, a strikingly patterned day flying species. It has a combination of iridescent bottle green

Above: A dark green fritillary feeding on a pyramidal orchid in the dunes at Burnham Overy.

Below: Two brown argus butterflies about to mate.

The caterpillars of cinnabar moths are a voracious devourer of ragwort.

or black forewings each bearing six red spots, a direct, bottom heavy almost bee-like flight and long black antennae and proboscis giving it quite an exotic appearance. It is a swift flier and has a huge appetite for nectar. A warm day on the dunes in July usually provides the ideal conditions to witness good numbers seeking out the flowers of sea holly and thistles.

Perhaps even more plentiful and equally as conspicuous are cinnabar moths. These share similar black and red markings to the burnet but they differ in having a vertical red line down the outside edge of each closed wing and two spots spaced out at each tip. Resting by day in the depths of the dune's grasses, if disturbed they will soon fly off with a slow fluttering, laboured flight. These moths are on the wing from late April but their presence is heightened even more in July when their characteristic yellow and black-banded caterpillars festoon the abundant flush of yellow ragwort flowers.

A broad-bordered bee hawk-moth.   *A hummingbird hawk-moth.*

A bedstraw hawk-moth feeding on pink campion at Holkham in June 1996, on one of its rare visits.

One of North Norfolk's most prized creatures is the natterjack toad.

There are two sites along our coast that are home to a much localised amphibian. The shallow pools in the dune slacks at Holkham and Holme are the favoured habitat of the natterjack toad. This is another jewel in the crown of North Norfolk and a species with such particular habitat requirements that it remains scarce throughout most of England.

Natterjack toads are slightly smaller than their common cousins and with their blotchy green/grey/brown colouration, a yellow back stripe, orange tipped body warts and green irises are altogether showier looking creatures. Despite their mixture of colours they can be notoriously difficult to see. During the winter they hibernate either in holes in the sand or under old logs or masonry, before emerging in the spring when they return to traditional pools to breed. These are unshaded, shallow, sandy bottomed and prone to dry out in particularly hot summers. Common toads often shun such uncertain and temporary conditions but if they do arrive, problems arise for the natterjack's offspring, as life becomes difficult competing with larger tadpoles. To its advantage, the natterjack possesses adaptations that make it a more successful inhabitant of the dunes. The skin on its underparts is highly absorbent, which allows it to take in fluid from a minute covering of surface water, while the regular habit of burrowing into the sand enables it to draw goodness from moisture below the ground. So while drought may prevent successful breeding one year, the toad's ability to survive sometimes for many years, at least enables future attempts to be made when conditions once more become suitable.

Natterjacks are primarily nocturnal but on warm days in the spring or after breeding in late summer they can sometimes be encountered on the move, wandering through exposed patches of sand in the dunes. With hind legs shorter than those of a common toad, the natterjack has a very distinctive, fast moving crawl. If caught unawares out on open ground it is quite surprising how swiftly it will move to get to safety and if persistently harassed it is not unusual for the toad to bury itself into the sand. Such nifty movements led it to become known as the 'running toad' in years gone by.

When the returning males arrive to their chosen breeding pool, they begin to advertise their presence with a loud purring 'song' hoping to attract females so spawning can begin. This usually commences at the end of April and can last for up to six weeks. Whilst this far reaching communal chorus is normally carried out from dusk onwards on still nights, odd bursts of song sometimes break out during the day on hot or showery days. Approach a favoured pool with care and it is sometimes possible to witness a male natterjack with his bluish throat sack fully inflated as he proclaims his territory with bizarre vocalisations. Once the female has selected and mated with her chosen songster, single strings of tiny black eggs are laid, which after a period of four to eight weeks will have progressed into tiny toadlets.

Despite the Natterjack's hardy and resilient nature it is a sad fact that it is becoming an exceptionally rare creature. Within the last hundred years the British population has declined by 75%, making the North Norfolk colonies a valuable outpost in need of preservation. The disappearance of once viable populations has been caused by many reasons. Coastal sites have been lost where dunes have been developed as both golf courses and holiday complexes while scrub encroachment around pools and forestation has caused further losses. Natterjacks once favoured many heaths in the south and east of England and indeed North Norfolk has one such ancient population left at Syderstone Common. Numbers here have been constantly dwindling and despite efforts by the Norfolk Wildlife Trust to enhance the habitat, it seems that extinction there may not be far away.

A displaying male natterjack with his throat sack fully extended.

Roosting knot congregate on the smallest patches of the beach at high water.

Chapter Three

A beach full of birds

For most of North Norfolk's visitors, the nearest they get to its wide-open spaces are its beaches. Places like Holkham, Wells and Brancaster positively buzz with the bustle of crowds enjoying the coast on a hot summer's day.

The winter months by contrast, create an entirely different view and ambience. Sometimes a fierce northerly gale roars in off the sea with a chill that leaves no doubt it is coming straight from the Arctic. Waves crash into the dunes often carving out a cliff-like edge. Sand is deposited, sculpted by the wind and the sea only to be eroded away by winter storms. It is a harsh environment that on occasion seems an empty place devoid of life but nothing could be further from the truth. North Norfolk's beaches in the winter may sometimes lack the human factor but they often host an even larger array of life than can be seen trooping onto the sands at Holkham on a hot August bank holiday.

By November the nesting terns will have gone, vacating our shoreline for the warmer waters of the West African coast. In their place there will be another fascinating band of travelling birds, some from nesting grounds within the British Isles, others from as far away as Scandinavia, Greenland, arctic Canada and Siberia. Waders and wildfowl descend in great numbers to make North Norfolk an internationally important destination as they migrate each autumn to escape an inhospitable winter in their northern breeding grounds.

Three things provide the attraction; solitude, space and food, and all can be found on this coast in the winter. Thanks to the intricate physical structure of the salt marshes and the dangers of tidal creeks, many places are only accessible to human intrusion when the tide is at its lowest. Over the years the marshes have claimed many a careless victim and consequently such places are hardly overrun with people. They are pretty much left for nature to go about its daily routines, free from disturbance.

With the sea washing over the area twice a day, it is inhabited by a large diversity of life, much of which provides a welcome source of food for birds. Walk the tideline at low water and this variety instantly becomes apparent. Razor shells and starfish may be in abundance one day, jellyfish, bladder wrack along with empty cockle and mussel shells or cuttlefish 'bone', another. Anything that lives or has lived in the sea (or that mankind has dumped into it) can be found on the beach. Anything is possible, from the corpses of seals, dolphins and sea birds stricken by famine or pollution far out at sea to the bloated, bizarre shape of a sun fish, a species usually more at home in warmer waters. Such sights give but a mere hint of the rich diversity of life that is present not far from our shores.

One creature that remains very rare in Britain yet has been washed ashore in North Norfolk on five occasions between 1986 and 2006 is the mighty sperm whale. Frequently reaching 50 feet in length and weighing over 50 tons there is little wonder every appearance guarantees a crowd of admirers. These impressive giants are normally encountered in the southern oceans, although males (which all the modern ones have been) are known to live a solitary, wandering existence. In more historical times there is a very intriguing record from 1646, when 'one or more' were beached at Holme, another at Wells, with eight or nine cast ashore nearby including two with calves.

This enormous sperm whale was washed up dead on the beach at Stiffkey in April 2003.

Holkham beach after northerly winds have washed ashore a vast carpet of razor shells.

Much of what is washed up along our tideline can and will be exploited by hungry avian eyes and bills, yet it is the commoner every day life forms of the intertidal mud flats and marshes that become the main focus for the wintering birds. Beneath the mud there is an abundance of invertebrate life such as bivalve molluscs (the common cockle being the most recognisable), lugworms and ragworms and minute snails called spire-snails. Thousands of tiny shore and sand hoppers inhabit the tideline debris while temporary tidal pools might harbour shore crabs and sand eels.

Waders and wildfowl are among the most numerous groups of birds that winter on our coast and consequently are difficult to miss. Some species are content to feed in places close to human activity in the various harbours and tidal channels where they ignore our comings and goings while others prefer the wide-open spaces of the foreshore, where for the most part they can feed free of disturbance. Many species utilise these areas but there is one that prefers this environment to anywhere else. The knot really is the bird most associated with this open and bleak landscape. Always at the mercy of the weather and under threat from a small winter population of peregrine falcons, the key to survival for the knot really is safety in numbers.

The first migrants return in July and August from their nesting grounds on the remote tundra lands of Greenland and the high arctic of eastern Canada. At first they are in their fine brick red breeding colours but by the end of September most will be in their more indistinct non-breeding grey brown plumage. During the following months until March, numbers reach their peak and it is then that their great character becomes most apparent enhanced by the spectacular size of the flocks that they form. The Wash has traditionally been a home for internationally important numbers of knot and it is certainly the most favoured feeding and roosting ground in East Anglia. The coastal flats between Wells and Stiffkey are also attractive, albeit to a smaller number and here they feast on cockles and another similar but smaller shell

fish, the Baltic tellin. Sandwiched between these two areas is the Holme-Hunstanton stretch of coast. This frequently holds large numbers of knot, particularly during high tides when birds from the Wash are often forced eastwards to Gore Point at Holme and sometimes even to the lagoons at the RSPB's Titchwell reserve where they can roost in peace.

Gore Point produced North Norfolk's largest number of knot when up to 200,000 birds were estimated there on October 16th 1993, a count that has yet to be surpassed. Here they can often be seen packed onto what appears far too small an area to accommodate such huge numbers. They huddle together, some sleeping, others preening or hopping about on one leg and jostling their neighbours for a better spot. And after what seems like far too short a roosting period, the flock will be up and away, bursting into life in a magical blur of swirling flight formations. As they twist and turn in complete unison, like a single living, moving organism, the flock takes on a multitude of bewildering forms.

Sanderlings are another species perfectly at home on the foreshore. Smaller than a knot and immaculate in their pale winter dress, they too breed in Greenland and Siberia but in the winter they prefer the water's edge of our sandy beaches. Here they scurry about in small groups, rushing to and fro between each breaking wave, methodically probing for food. Any number of items is devoured; small molluscs and crustaceans washed ashore, worms taken from below the mud, shore hoppers snatched from the sand's surface and even the seeds of samphire. One item that has attracted large numbers particularly to the sands of Holkham Bay at low water is the abundance of razor shells that is often found there.

Unlike the knot, there are never tens of thousands of sanderlings on our shores. A flock of 400 would be a good-sized group, and indeed sometimes the entire North Norfolk winter population may only reach 1000. Nevertheless the sanderling is very much part of the local scenery and between late departing birds in June and the first returning adults in July there is never a very long period when our tideline is not visited by these ever restless and charming birds.

A sanderling feeding on a razor shell.

The sanderling is commonly seen rushing to and fro to feed between each breaking wave.

Despite their size, small waders such as sanderling, dunlin and knot were once regularly sought as a valuable meat source. In the 1800s they were simply known as 'stints' and their meat was renowned for making good pies. So valued was the income that as well as shooting these waders, long lines of nets were erected across the mud flats to catch passing flocks. Such measures might sound barbaric today but in the past any way to earn a living or put food on the table was necessary to survive. Indeed there is a famous tale of three Blakeney wildfowlers who in February 1901 simultaneously shot their punt guns into a group of about 4000 waders at Stiffkey and killed 603 knot, 9 redshanks and 6 dunlin. One of the same men on another occasion fired a gun three times into a flock, bringing down 120 knot in the process.

Other waders of the mud flats such as grey plovers can be rather tamer than the restless flocks of knot, if feeding in the channels at places such as Wells, Thornham and Burnham Overy where they become accustomed to the presence of people. Here grey plovers can be watched hauling out worms grabbed from just below the surface of the mud, just as happily infact as out on the mudflats of the Wash, the most important site for them in Britain. As many as 1600 may be scattered along this coast, small numbers in comparison to the 11,000 sometimes present in the Wash, but North Norfolk is still an area that is nationally important for the species.

Grey plovers may look sombre in their rather nondescript grey spangled winter plumage yet they are still just as fascinating to watch. They either run or walk in a determined fashion, before suddenly stopping and remaining motionless, head angled to the side, waiting for the slightest movement to snatch a meal with a determined grab of their stout bills. In food rich tidal creeks and channels it is not unusual to see these birds spaced out every few yards. They seem to occupy their own little territory, which they fiercely defend from each other. Grey plovers are also quite crafty. Very often a smaller bird such as a turnstone will struggle to catch and prise open a shore crab, only for a plover to rush across and snatch the precious innards.

A high tide wader roost complete with knot, sanderling, turnstone, grey plovers and dunlin.

Prolonged spells of long and penetrating frosts can lead to our tidal creeks and mud flats freezing over with a thick crust of ice. It might be an uncommon occurrence these days, yet if it does happen it can be disastrous for our wintering waders. Feeding opportunities dwindle and the inevitable fatalities begin. Grey plovers and redshank are among the worst hit species in such times. In recent years 1991 stands out when as many up to 2500 wader corpses were found in the Norfolk section of the Wash and North Norfolk alone (918 from Holme to Scolt Head). Up to 1356 redshanks, 519 dunlin and 354 grey plovers came from this total. The long drawn out winter of 1963 must have been even worse. Although no figures are available, evidence suggests fatalities were on an even greater scale, with the redshank population said to be have been decimated. Some starving dunlin and knot were even witnessed at Wells being openly attacked by equally hungry water rails, birds that are renowned for usually shunning such an open environment. Even the secretive woodcock, an incredibly shy wader of our woodlands, was forced to feed out on the few ice-free tidal channels, some so weak that they were incapable of flying.

By April and May most of the wintering waders will have gone, although notable numbers from wintering grounds further south also pass through. This is then the time to seek out grey plovers in their immaculate black and white summer plumage. Similarly, bar-tailed godwits are moving back to their nesting grounds in Scandinavia and northern Russia and they too will be in fine plumage, a beautiful brick red colouration, stretching from head to vent. They are shorter legged and have plainer wings than the similar black-tailed godwit that now occurs in ever increasing numbers in North Norfolk. Bar-tailed godwits are also much more at home on the sea shore, in muddy creeks and tidal channels.

Right: Worm casts on the mud flats at Wells Harbour.

The bar-tailed godwit plunges its bill deep in the mud to find a plentiful supply of worms.

Like the grey plover, the bar-tailed godwit adopts a grey-brown winter plumage and also flocks to the Wash in large numbers. Again this is the most important British site for this species but during particularly high tides a number of bar-tailed godwits will fly along the coast to places such as Holme, Thornham and Titchwell RSPB reserve. A count of over 5000 was made at the latter site in October 1990, the largest of recent years. Smaller numbers can be found at all the other north coast harbours and flocks of several hundred frequently feed on the mud flats east of Wells.

Bar-tailed godwits can also become exceptionally confiding and they can often be watched probing deep into the mud with their long, slightly up curved bills, in search of lug and rag worms that are swiftly consumed when found. Their long bills enable them to find worms that many of the shorter billed waders cannot reach and they can be seen plunging them so deep into the oozy mud that occasionally their heads may also disappear momentarily. Sometimes they may be feeding solitarily, but find them out on a quiet piece of shoreline and they are bound to be in a tight pack. Here they will be energetically feeding, often surrounded by worm casts on the mud's surface that give a good clue as to what they are after.

The mud flats and beaches of North Norfolk are thought of as being primarily the haunt of wading birds, yet there is often a very good chance of connecting with the odd roving flock of small passerines such as shore larks or snow buntings in the winter.

Shore larks have a wholly unique appearance in Britain, with yellow and black face markings and tiny 'devil-like' horn shaped feathering on their crowns. They can be found nesting across much of North America, central Asia, northern and central Europe and even in the Atlas Mountains of North Africa. Our wintering birds, it seems, are most likely to originate from the tundra and mountain tops of Scandinavia and northern Russia and usually arrive in October-November. They are wonderfully charismatic little birds, always busy running and foraging through the debris left after high tides or amidst the developing salt marsh vegetation in search of the seeds of plants such as samphire, annual sea-blite, sea purslane or sea aster, though any chance encounter with insect prey will be quickly snapped up.

It could be said that Norfolk has always had strong links with the shore lark as the first British specimen was obtained at Sheringham back in 1830. Since then, the species has enjoyed mixed fortunes progressing from relatively common winter visitor in the 1890s when Pashley, the Cley taxidermist, had them brought to his shop by the dozen, to a very lean spell in the 1980s when only a handful were recorded annually. By the 1990s numbers had once more begun to rise and they reached an unprecedented peak in 1998 when the largest recorded British influx occurred. North Norfolk produced the most, with up to 534 individuals counted during a co-ordinated count while a single flock of 240 at Holkham on November 24th was by far the biggest group ever recorded in the British Isles.

The shore lark is a winter visitor from the mountains of northern Europe.

The sight of an ever-mobile flock of snow buntings wheeling around like an unexpected snow flurry is another highlight on the beaches in the winter months. They are, however, far more widely dispersed around Britain than shore larks and even nest regularly on the highest tops of Scotland's highlands. Although they breed in a very wide circumpolar sweep, ringing data has proven that most of North Norfolk's wintering birds originate from Iceland along with smaller numbers of Scandinavian and even Greenland origin.

Flock numbers have traditionally been much higher than shore larks, with as many as 200 to 300 being nothing unusual, although groups at Cley, Stiffkey and Holkham have occasionally reached 500. Despite being associated with the coast, snow buntings can venture inland, sometimes to bathe in the fresh water of adjacent meadows, or to exploit new feeding grounds on arable or stubble fields.

Another species, the twite, used to frequently be seen feeding alongside snow buntings and shore larks. These small, tawny finches with stubby yellow bills, nest in the Pennines and up until the early 1990s, flocks of 500 were frequent in the winter months along the coast. Since then there has been a drastic decline, with only two or three groups of less than 100 birds appearing annually since the new millennium. One reason for their disappearance has been a dramatic fall in breeding numbers. Research has shown that changing farming practises combined closely with the twite's specialised diet has caused the decline. Unlike most small seed eating birds that feed their chicks on insects, young twite actually survive on seeds. Due to many meadows being cut for silage early in the season instead of being left for hay, feeding opportunities have greatly diminished.

Above: Snow buntings winter in Norfolk and in the past were referred to as 'snowflakes' by locals.

Below: The car park beside the shingle ridge at Salthouse is one of the area's best snow bunting sites.

One of the coast's greatest spectacles is the enormous numbers of pinkfeet flying to roost.

There is one other winter gathering of birds which arguably provides the ultimate local wildlife spectacle. This is the huge numbers of pink-footed geese that arrive annually to seek respite from an unforgiving winter in the Icelandic lava flows and the tundra of Greenland where they nest each summer. We will look more closely at them later, but there can be no description of the shoreline in winter without mentioning the 'pinkfeet' (an abbreviation they have acquired over the years). After feeding by day on adjacent grazing marshes or inland on harvested sugar beet fields, the geese join together at dusk and make their way to roosting areas on the sands and mud flats of traditional undisturbed beaches.

In North Norfolk we have two very special places for pinkfeet: Scolt Head Island and the sands between Wells and Stiffkey. Both are remote, vast in their extent and generally free from disturbance, ideal in every way for the roosting geese. Further around the coast, the shore of the Wash at Snettisham also attracts large numbers and depending on where the inland feeding is taking place, there will be a progressive switch as to which roosting area is favoured. A new site on the foreshore at Thornham was used in 2002 and 2003 by a smaller number than at the three main sites.

As we shall see later, the fortunes of the pinkfeet have changed dramatically since the 1980s, with enormous numbers currently spending their winters here. Between 2003 and 2007 over 100,000 were counted, making our area one of the most important wintering grounds anywhere in the world.

It is a wonderful experience to witness pinkfeet feeding, but to watch their clamorous flights at dusk or their early morning exodus is to see them at their most awe inspiring. Waiting for these special moments will fill the observer with great anticipation. The cold air, the magical mix of colours in the sky along with the panorama of the view from whichever marsh side point the great battalion of birds passes over, all add to the atmosphere.

Often the first sign that they are coming are distant cackles and yelps but as they draw close, it turns into a musical cacophony, far different from the farmyard goose-like honking of the resident greylag geese. As the noise reaches a climax, the sky overhead will be darkened with long lines of well defined 'v' formations and skeins following one after the other and gradually merging into an immense mass of rushing wings. All the while anxious calling fills the air until the flock has passed over only to be followed minutes later by yet more geese. After all too short a time, their calls fade into the distance and an over riding calm returns to the marsh. As many as 50,000 geese may have passed over, to pack themselves tightly onto a distant flat of sand for the night or, by day, to take over a suitable sugar beet field maybe as far as ten miles away.

Such an experience can leave you strangely numb and empty when the excitement is over and an eerie silence returns to the marsh. Generations of writers and artists have celebrated North Norfolk's pinkfeet while wildfowlers past and present have always had the species enshrined in their folklore. Indeed, for anyone remotely interested in wildlife and wild places, this mass movement of pinkfeet is without doubt the finest spectacle the North Norfolk coast in the winter can offer.

Pinkfeet on their evening flight over Wells Quay, en route to their roost at Warham.

The marshes at Wells are a purple haze of sea lavender in the height of summer.

Chapter Four

The salt marsh coast

Of all North Norfolk's habitats, its salt marshes are arguably its most revered. With an almost continuous stretch between Cley and Holme (broken only between Wells and Burnham Overy) it is one of Western Europe's largest and finest examples of an environment laid down by the actions of the sea. Its impact has been so significant to the area's character that some simply refer to North Norfolk as 'the salt marsh coast'.

In the simplest of explanations, salt marshes are formed by the continuous actions of the tide depositing and shifting silty sediments on extensive sand flats over a lengthy period of time. Gradually, higher areas are built up and stabilized by specialized salt-water tolerant plants while lower, sheltered areas will form into sinuous tidal creeks and channels. Salt marshes in their infancy may fluctuate in growth and appearance due to fragility ensured by tidal currents, yet the appearance of North Norfolk's coast is a great testament to what nature can produce if left unhindered. Such processes have been working over a long time scale along the North Norfolk coast and analysis of some of the coast's mud has shown that the salt marshes at Warham and Stiffkey may be over a thousand years old. And their evolution is still very much an ongoing process. There are newer examples too. At Holkham Gap the sand flats on the landward side of the outer dunes have, over a 20 year period beginning in the 1980s, developed into one of the finest examples of pioneering salt marsh along the whole coast. It could be that as the future unfolds, even more areas will revert to salt marsh. It is widely believed that rising sea levels will eventually result in much low lying land being reclaimed by the sea. With a cessation of regular strengthening of the shingle bank between Salthouse and Cley it is probably only a matter of time before that area once more becomes a tidal wetland.

From fledgling mud flats, marshes were formed and stabilized; some tidal creeks became navigable channels leading to sheltered marsh harbours that in turn did much to create greater access, trade and wealth within the area. Indeed all the villages along the coast were built up around harbours. Not only was the fishing industry able to thrive, but exports of wool and barley left our shores while imports of wheat, coal and timber were inward bound. Even villages up stream along the rivers Glaven and Stiffkey such as Letheringsett and Warham hosted busy ports in the middle ages.

Unfortunately man's actions eventually took their toll. With large areas of marsh embanked and claimed from the sea between the 1600s and 1800s, it was little wonder that the remaining channels silted up badly with the excess of sediments still being shifted and deposited twice daily by the tide. Many of the harbours became navigable only to the smallest of vessels, whilst some such as Holkham, Stiffkey and Wiveton were cut off from the sea completely due to the building of sea walls. Continual silting of the remaining channels and the arrival of the railway to Wells in 1857 effectively signalled a death knell for most of the area's coastal trade. The result was that Burnham Overy Staithe, Blakeney and Cley (by then the only viable ports aside from Wells) were to cease trading. Wells was able to continue to export grain and import fertilizers, soya and animal products until the late 1980s. In 1997 the Dutch sailing vessel, known as The Albatros (now permanently moored in the quay) delivered its last cargo and since then, due to the state of the channel, any other trading coasters have been unable to enter the harbour. Today, with the quayside grain silos long empty and converted to flats, all that remains of this once bustling port is a small fishing fleet, itself vulnerable due to over fishing in the past and even stricter regulations on just about all aspects of the industry. These days the harbours of North Norfolk are as much a haven for sailing boats as anything else.

Mussel grading at Overy Staithe channel.

Sea thrift is the first blaze of colour to enliven the salt marshes in late spring.

The one thing that the harbours and salt marshes have retained is their wildlife. As we have seen the birdlife of the marshes alone makes them nationally important, although with a cursory glance this may not always be apparent. More obvious to the first time visitor perhaps will be the variety of unfamiliar flora that covers the marsh. This too is an important component of this valuable habitat with some species found at very few other sites in Britain.

One of the species to create the first flush of colour in the spring is the sea-pink or thrift; it covers the higher reaches of the marsh in great profusion. As it passes its best in June, the emerging mauve flowers of common sea lavender replace it. This species really is a salt marsh specialist and, at its peak in July, almost the whole marsh becomes a huge swathe of mauve and lilac stretching to the horizon. It is the most abundant species of a family that also includes the nationally rare lax-flowered sea lavender. It inhabits only a few sites on the muddy inter-tidal zone where it is found alongside samphire and annual seablite. Rock sea lavender grows more abundantly along the edges of the marshes where sand and shingle form a firmer base while the smaller and more delicate matted sea lavender can be found at a handful of spots along the coast where sand, shingle and *suaeda* bushes meet. It is a lower growing species that is easily recognisable, as by the time it is in flower, its leaves have already withered away. Being primarily a Mediterranean species, its British range is almost exclusive to North Norfolk. Along with the ubiquitous *suaeda*, matted sea lavender and the tiny sea heath with its inconspicuous pink flowers, form part of a plant community that is unique to North Norfolk.

One of the finest times to enjoy the marshes is at the height of summer, when the lavender is at its best and a variety of insects are exploiting its abundance. Beekeepers often move their hives to the edge of the marsh, allowing the bees to capitalize on the availability of lavender nectar. Migrant silver-y moths have the same motive, while butterflies such as small and Essex skippers can often be seen as they too make the most of such bountiful feeding. Both species are orange, tiny and superficially very similar in appearance. The best way of telling them apart is the completely jet black bulbs on the end of each antenna of the Essex skipper; those of the small skippers have brownish yellow undersides. The small skipper *(see page 115)* has always been common here but since the 1990s its similar relative has become equally abundant.

Suaeda bushes and matted sea lavender at Burnham Overy.

Sea heath is a national rarity that grows at the drier edges of salt marshes.

Below: The Essex skipper is frequently attracted to flowering sea lavender.

'Samphire' beds on the lower reaches of the salt marsh at Morston.

Also characteristic of the salt marshes are the subtly different glasswort species, more commonly referred to as 'samphire'. Small and succulent, it is a favoured local food source and grows in areas of pioneering marsh where the mud flats are frequently submerged by the tide. Although at its best for eating in mid summer when it is a vibrant translucent green, samphire later takes on a multitude of rich orange and red colours when gone to seed in the autumn. Catch it in the right light and the blaze of colour almost equals that of autumn beech trees.

Sea purslane is another common salt marsh plant; its rubbery pastel green leaves forming continuous mats that overhang the creek edges while the taller, frailer and fragrant smelling sea wormwood often grows nearby. Their blooms are quite unimpressive and could easily be overlooked, unlike sea aster which flowers later in September. Resembling Michaelmas daisies, sea aster flower heads are a mixture of yellow (central 'cushions' of disc-florets), and pale purple (outer fringes of petal-like ray-florets). Throughout most of the salt marshes, particularly in areas regularly inundated by the tide, sea asters are found in a form that lack the purple ray florets. They grow in such densities that in the autumn, the purple haze of sea lavender is replaced by the warm yellow hues of sea aster

Sea asters in full flower.

Above: The salt marshes are a warm yellow when sea aster flowers at the end of the summer.

Below: Salt marsh creeks such as this one at Burnham Deepdale are a haven for wintering waders and wildfowl.

A winter gathering of redshanks.

One of the most obvious birds of the marsh is the redshank. Although it is thought of as being a resident, like many other waders, it has more complex migratory movements amidst its widespread population. Breeding birds from as far north as Iceland migrate south to moult and winter in both Britain and Europe, often joining our resident birds, (which are thought not to migrate far) while others that nest eastwards from Scandinavia into Russia undoubtedly pass through *en route* to wintering grounds in West Africa. The wintering population of redshanks along the North Norfolk coast generally averages at a peak of about 1700 birds in most winters, although a dedicated search of all suitable habitat in November 1997 revealed 3556 birds spread out between Holme and Weybourne.

In the spring the male redshank commonly undertakes a fast rising, yodelling song flight. He rises up, bill wide open, quivering his wings rapidly before gliding with wings held out and tail splayed, and then gently descending to the ground. Prior to mating he approaches the female, head bent forward, bill pointing down but open, excitedly calling to her with wings held arched and outwards. These are quivered so rapidly that as he gets closer, he starts to leave the ground. If she is submissive and responsive he then hovers over her back before mating. As they part company, both call triumphantly as they run off, bodies bent forward with tails spread, the male still excitedly fluttering his wings.

When on the nest the sitting hen is easy to miss, usually preferring deep grass tussocks where it remains well hidden. Redshanks nest throughout the upper reaches of the marsh amongst the salt marsh grasses and underneath the lines of *suaeda* bushes where they are safe from all but the highest of tides. Some even make their nests close to the high water mark amongst the tidal debris that accumulates there while others have been known to make their shallow depression under tussocks of marram and sea couch grass on the newer dune systems that are always springing up close to the shore in undisturbed places such as Morston and Stiffkey. Such birds have to constantly deal with the great hazard of tidal flooding. North Norfolk's population averages about 200 to 300 nesting pairs, yet even here there have been periodic declines. Numbers were said to be so poor in the mid 1800s that the commercial gathering of redshanks eggs from the salt marshes and their subsequent selling on Norwich market came to an end.

Another bird commonly encountered on the salt marshes is the curlew. Its evocative disyllabic calls are as much a part of the North Norfolk coast as they are of the moors of upland Britain where many nest. Not that all the birds we encounter originate there as it seems that most are of Scandinavian origin. Here they nest in open forest bogs, high moorland, wet meadows and rough pasture.

June signals the arrival of many female curlews in Norfolk. Having hatched their offspring, they depart from Scandinavia, leaving their mates to continue with parental duties before they too migrate south. As autumn continues our marshes begin to fill with large flocks. Many arrive, pausing to moult, before continuing to the shores of Africa, while others will spend the remainder of the winter in Norfolk; the last birds departing again by mid May.

The familiar impression of a curlew in the winter is often that of a solitary bird standing huddled in a saltpan or wandering back and forth along a stretch of salt-water channel ever on the look out for a crab or worm to feed on. Yet curlews are far from being loners. Watch from a distance at Brancaster, Wells or Blakeney as a low flying aeroplane passes overhead and the air will positively echo to the familiar cries of curlews as groups sometimes into their hundreds arise from hidden creeks and muddy corners of the marshes. In the winter larger groups can frequently be seen inland, feeding on earth worms in fields of winter wheat and barley. They congregate in a loose flock sometimes over a hundred strong, feeding all day until darkness draws near and then they return to the coast to spend the night.

The curlew is a great lover of crabs that it finds in the muddy creeks.

The rock pipit is an inconspicuous yet common winter visitor to the salt marshes.

The rock pipit is one species that lives almost exclusively on the salt marshes when it winters in North Norfolk. Despite being quite common, because it lurks in the creeks and is a rather drab dark, streaky songbird it is often over looked. Sometimes it seems there are a dozen in even the smallest of creeks and when a series of counts carried out in 1997 found that over 3000 were present between Holme and Cley it came as little surprise. Frequenting the furthest reaches of the salt marshes, rock pipits can also be seen well in the harbours where they often become confiding, freely perching on moored boats. Unlike the meadow pipit which it superficially resembles, the rock pipit does not nest in Norfolk, instead favouring the rocky coasts of Scandinavia.

Oystercatchers are also just at home in the harbours, particularly at Brancaster Staithe, where local fishermen sort and grade mussels from lays in the nearby harbour mouth. Here oystercatchers can be seen using their bright red bills to either smash or prize open a shell. Others will be rushing about with a shell in their bill, eager for a feast before a rival nips in to steal the precious contents. Another bird that frequently feeds on mussels is the herring gull. Without as potent a tool as the oystercatcher's bill, the herring gull resorts to a different tactic. It flies up into the air, complete with mussel, before dropping it down onto hard ground in anticipation that the shell will break. It will then drop down for its meal, that is, if it can beat the turnstones that are always waiting to steal a gull's hard earned food. Turnstones may be opportunists but they certainly thrive, surviving in hard weather when other species find it difficult to feed in the frozen creeks. When the port of Wells was in its heyday turnstones used to feed on spilt grain and soya although since then bread thrown out for gulls and even discarded fish and chips provide just as welcoming a source of nutrition. In such environments turnstones not surprisingly become very tame.

Turnstones are of course just as likely to be seen feeding along the tideline of our beaches where they can be seen amidst the flotsam left by high tides. Their bills have evolved enabling them to flip over stones, pebbles, strands of seaweed or any other item of tidal debris that they comes across as they scour the strand at low water in search of shore crabs, tiny *hydrobia* snails, sand hoppers, or any other small mollusc or invertebrate. Such behaviour gave the Turnstone the very endearing old Norfolk name of the 'tangle-picker'. Another local name was the

Mussel heaps at Brancaster Harbour are a favoured feeding area for the turnstone.

'sea-dotterel', presumably due to its close association with the shoreline. Turnstones are present at most coastal localities in the winter although Brancaster and Scolt Head remain the favoured haunts for the biggest concentrations and it is the mussels that provide the attraction. Many can often be seen roosting at high water on the moored boats that line the harbour and channel, though counts of 600 back in February and December of 1968 have yet to be beaten. By May all but a few will have departed to breeding grounds in Greenland, Northern Canada, Russia and islands in the Baltic Sea.

A flock of turnstones roosting on a 'Brancaster flat',
a unique boat designed for mussel gathering in the harbour there.

As well as providing an ideal feeding area for many wading birds, North Norfolk's harbours often offer a sanctuary for wintering sea ducks, divers and grebes as well as the more typical wildfowl. Some species such as little grebes maintain a constant presence in the winter yet may have only moved from nearby breeding localities. By contrast, the scarcer black-necked, slavonian or red-necked grebes are birds that appear midwinter if the Baltic Sea freezes over. Cormorants are very much part of the scenery, always diving for flat fish or resting with wet wings out stretched. Their smaller, sleeker relative, the shag also puts in appearances with small numbers roosting occasionally on quayside buildings at Wells and moored boats in Brancaster Channel. More readily identifiable is the kingfisher. Although generally a shy and solitary bird that nests alongside the rivers inland, with patience it can frequently be seen in the harbours along the coast in the autumn and winter. Here it perches up on boats and sluice gates waiting to catch any small fish or crustacean from the water below.

Kingfishers are most frequently observed on the coast in the autumn and winter months.

One duck commonly encountered at sea in the winter, yet also seen in the harbours is the red-breasted merganser. Drakes are resplendent with a spiky crested, bottle green head and a red, narrow bill. Equally as handsome and perhaps more likely to be seen at close quarters is the goldeneye. On fine sunny days, if there are two or three males present alongside a drabber female, display by the amorous drakes will occur. Flinging their heads back and rising up from the water with chests puffed out, before dipping their bills into the water they then launch themselves at the female, sometimes uttering strange guttural calls. Despite such behaviour being reasonably easy to observe, goldeneyes do not nest here. By April they will be gone proclaiming a territory on some secluded woodland pool deep in the highlands of Scotland or Scandinavia.

Above: A drake goldeneye about to eat a crab.

Below: Flocks of brent geese are a regular winter sight in Wells harbour.

Fresh water springs in the harbours offer brent geese a regular chance to bathe after feeding.

Far more conspicuous are the brent geese that arrive to make the salt marshes and harbours their temporary home. The brent geese, which are widespread during the winter in North Norfolk, are of the dark bellied sub-species that nest in the coastal tundra and offshore islets and rivers of northern Russia and east into the Taimyr Peninsula of Siberia.

The first brents usually appear in Norfolk by early to mid September, vanguards for the bulk of the population that arrive in late October-November. Up until the mid 1990s our coastal marshes held a combined total that sometimes reached 14,000 birds although numbers have appeared to be dwindling quite noticeably since the new millennium with counts scarcely averaging 7000 birds. Populations do have a habit of varying dramatically, due to the success or failure of the breeding season. When the youngsters appear with their parents in North Norfolk, they are easily recognisable by the obvious white fringes on their wings and they also initially lack the pale neck collar of the adult birds. In good years the fruits of a highly productive nesting season can be seen, with family groups of four or five youngsters being commonplace amongst the flocks, while other years there will be no young present. Such failure years are attributed to a lack of rodent prey on the tundra forcing predators such as arctic foxes to prey upon the contents of a goose nest instead of lemmings and voles that are generally favoured.

Like most geese in the winter, brents are highly gregarious and small parties or sometimes large flocks are commonly found scattered along stretches of the upper marsh at low water, grazing on the salt marsh grasses. In the past the brent geese were almost exclusively a maritime species, feeding in the harbours and on the saltings but several factors have altered their habits. The long ribbon-like strands of eel-grass that formerly flourished in the tidal shallows along the coast was once the staple diet of the geese, but a catastrophic decline in the plant's fortunes in the 1930s was at least partly responsible for both a switch in diet and a population crash shown by the brent. The first returning geese manage to seek out patches of narrow-leaved and dwarf eel-grass that still grow in traditional spots but they are soon forced to find more plentiful alternatives. Another coastal food is the commonly encountered green alga *enteromorpha* although since the late twentieth century brents have increasingly relied upon coastal grassland such as meadows, golf courses and football pitches along with autumn sown cereal crops up to a few miles inland, something that would have been quite unthinkable in the past.

Of all the birds that are encountered on the salt marshes, the little egret is one that never quite looks at home. This gleaming white member of the heron family, with its bright yellow feet and fancy plumes adorning its head and back, looks positively alien in its choice of habitat. Nothing, however, could be further from the truth. Despite appearing far more suited to the Mediterranean coast or an African lake shore, it has arrived here in ever increasing numbers since the mid 1990s to become firmly established in North Norfolk. Yet between the region's first recorded sighting (at Cley) in 1952 and 1988 there were only 26 seen in the whole of Norfolk. Amazingly numbers increased to such a level that the species became an all year round resident that nested for the first time in Norfolk in 2002. From an initial five nests in an area of dense swampy woodland at Holkham, the population rapidly grew to 14 pairs in 2003, increasing to almost 60 pairs by 2008.

An expanding population in France and Spain triggered by milder winters has been mooted as the reason for colonisation and there is no denying that the species has found and exploited a niche with little competition. The first two birds wintered in 1994 in the Stiffkey-Warham area, where they spent their time fishing the small pools that remain full of water (and life) even at low water. Here they fed on a multitude of small fish and crabs with only the odd grey heron or curlew for competition. The very fact that there is such a wealth of these well-stocked pools

The sole North Norfolk breeding colony of little egrets.

Little egrets have gone from being great rarities to easily observed and plentiful.

in such a large area has obviously been the key to the egret's rapid colonization.

The little egret is usually quite solitary as it feeds during the day on the salt marsh. Each egret usually avoids direct company when feeding, preferring to stake a saltpan as its own, sometimes fiercely defending it from a rival. Here they will stand, sometimes watching patiently for any signs of movement, other times shuffling their feet below the surface of the water in the hope of stirring up a potential prey item. At dusk the marsh comes alive with egrets as they all start to become restless, congregating in groups before heading off in ghostly white processions to their roosting grounds amidst the willows at Holkham. Sometimes groups of half a dozen will leave, other times tight bundles up to 70 birds strong have been seen. By the end of an evening flight well over 100 may have left the saltmarshes, although in the autumn months when numbers are at their peak after the breeding season over 250 have been counted. Smaller numbers also roost at Titchwell and in riverside willows at Stiffkey. Regardless of number, it always remains an impressive yet somewhat exotic sight.

The wide-open spaces of North Norfolk's coastal marshes are the favoured haunt of two of our most charismatic predators: the hen harrier and the short-eared owl. Small numbers arrive each autumn to spend the winter here. Birds from the continent appear as well as individuals from northern and western Britain where they nest on moors, in bogs and newly planted conifer plantations.

Short-eared owls love large areas of open, disturbance free habitat where they can hunt for their beloved small mammals. The sight of this long winged owl with its wonderfully, fluid almost elastic flight action, silently beating across the salt marshes is made all the more impressive when it draws near. It has fierce yellow eyes which set in their dark surrounding feathers give it an almost permanent look of anger.

In the past, the odd isolated pair of short-eared owls actually nested on the higher reaches of the salt marsh, but such occurrences are rare. When this has happened they have not been too welcome as prey items have included young terns from Blakeney Point. Migrant short-eared owls and their similar long-eared cousins, appear at coastal sites, sometimes in a state of exhaustion during northerly and easterly winds in October and early November. Such arrivals in the past often coincided with the appearance of woodcock from the continent, hence both species of owl became known to local wildfowlers as 'woodcock owls'. Numbers of short-eared owls usually remain low, although local plagues of voles or rats have in the past resulted in larger than normal numbers, as has a dearth of rodents in Scandinavia. In the 1960s roosts of a score or more were not infrequent, but since the 1980s, the numbers that appear during a North Norfolk winter, are much less. Fortunately the short-eared owl, unlike the long-eared, is a diurnal hunter and it is usually the easier species to observe.

Hen harriers cover vast distances on their daily routines and as well as hunting the salt marshes in search of small birds such as larks, buntings and pipits to prey on, they frequently fly inland in their quest for a meal. As dusk approaches, however, hen harriers leave the stubble and sugar beet fields behind and make a purposeful return to the coast where they gather at a handful of traditional sites. Although they are solitary hunters by day, at night they roost together. The majority head for two separate areas of salt marsh where they favour thickets of *suaeda* or beds of *spartina* grass to sleep in. In addition, one coastal reed bed and one of the heaths north east of Holt are also regularly used. Numbers are usually low at each site particularly the latter, although four or five are regular at the salt marsh sites, eight or nine exceptionally.

The diurnal hunting short-eared owl is best seen in the autumn and winter on the coastal marshes.

The grazing marshes at Burnham Norton, part of Holkham National Nature Reserve.

Chapter Five

Marshes made by man

Within North Norfolk's naturally rich habitats, there is one immensely important stretch of land that is essentially man made and managed yet has become home to a great number of birds. The fresh water grazing marshes with their reed beds and dyke networks offer the ideal environment for breeding birds such as lapwings, redshank, avocets, marsh harriers and snipe along with wigeon and wild geese in the winter. These marshes are even more important due to the loss of similar habitat and changes in land management elsewhere. The North Norfolk coast offers a lifeline to birds that would be hard pressed to exist in their current numbers anywhere else within not only our area but also in much of Norfolk.

Due to the march of agricultural progress through the nineteenth and twentieth centuries, many rough uncultivated meadows, damp riverside pastures and even the wettest of commons throughout the British Isles were lost to drainage and ultimately intensive farming. It was estimated that between 1930 and 1980 up to 40% of Britain's grassland disappeared. Birds like the snipe and lapwing were simply losing a race for survival. Even on their other traditional haunts like the flint strewn cultivated fields of our farmland, lapwings attempting to nest faced the threat of large agricultural machinery, intensive use of pesticides and herbicides and a switch from spring sown cereals to autumn sown crops, which made their existence ever more precarious. Avocets and marsh harriers, currently two of the coast's most conspicuous birds, were once far from common. They had never been as abundant as snipe and lapwings but what

A lapwing sitting tight on its nest.

few there were, soon dwindled to local extinction thanks to unjust pressure applied on them in the 1800s initially by egg and specimen collectors (*see chapter one*).

Since those far off dark days, North Norfolk's coast has become a place to be proud of. Its fresh water wetlands are now recognised as nationally important for breeding waders and internationally important for wintering wildfowl. They exist due to a series of changes to land management where constant attention to detail in water levels, predator control, mowing and grazing ensures that optimum conditions are maintained and bird populations sustained.

The story does not, however, start with today's well-managed grazing marshes. From the 1600s and 1700s when the agricultural revolution was in its infancy many attempts began to claim land from the sea. What once was an even more extensive network of salt marsh creeks and tidal channels became altered beyond all recognition due to a series of man made sea walls that decisively stopped the flow of the tide. All along the coast from Holme and Thornham in the west to Cley and Salthouse in the east, these former salt marshes were starved of their sea water and eventually dried out enough to become pasture land for cattle and sheep. More changes came around the Second World War when the demand for increased national food production triggered many landowners to drain even more of their meadows and cultivate them for arable farming. With this practise occurring all over the country there is little wonder that the numbers of nesting waders began to plummet. Nature, however, sometimes seems to come up with its own answers, none more so than the devastating floods that swamped East Anglia's coastline in 1953. The surge of sea water was so great that the aging sea walls could not hold back the fast rising flow of water. With much of the coast's fields and grazing meadows lying under a blanket of salt water for weeks, nature took hold again and many areas consequently remained as unimproved grass fields with damp margins, shallow pools in the remnants of the old salt marsh creeks and reed filled dykes and pools; in short the ideal habitat for flourishing numbers of wetland birds.

Apart from the changes that agriculture and unprecedented weather patterns forced onto the region, many improvements were instigated by conservation organisations. One of the prime sites on the coast today is Holkham, yet its success story is only a recent one. Despite almost 4000 hectares of Holkham and Crown estate land becoming in 1967 what was at that time England's second largest nature reserve, little was done to manage or enhance its fresh water habitat until English Nature's efforts at creating a wetland for birds in the 1980s and 1990s. Provision of sluices, culverts and pumps allowed the water table of Holkham's meadows to be effectively raised to within 10 cm of the surface while its dykes were grubbed out over a seven year rotation. This enabled a deeper level of water to be maintained with consequently more room for plant, invertebrate and bird life. Such measures combined with regular summer grazing from cattle on the meadows and a disturbance free zone during the nesting season and winter months has seen Holkham's wetland birds increase to beyond all expectation. Key species such as lapwings increased from 81 nesting pairs in 1986 to 355 in 2001, redshank went from eight breeding pairs in 1987 to 149 in 2001 and following the first nesting avocets in 1989, numbers had increased to 80 pairs by 2001. For a species once as widespread as the lapwing, whose numbers declined in England by 49% between 1987 and 2002 there is no denying just how important a place like Holkham has become. As with many sites that have undergone such noticeable changes, numbers of birds have levelled out from their peaks but there are still enough to ensure that the 900 hectares of Holkham's grazing marshes is one of lowland Britain's finest wet grassland sites.

The North Norfolk coast can boast more than one important wetland. In the west there is Holme, Titchwell and Brancaster while east of Wells there is Stiffkey, Blakeney, Salthouse and Kelling, yet the most long established and famous site is Cley Marsh. Within 180 hectares there is a wonderful mixture of fresh water and brackish pools, scrapes and extensive reed beds all overlooked by a series of well situated viewing hides and an impressive hill top visitor's centre.

A flock of avocets wheeling around over Cley Marsh.

Cley Marsh was the first wetland nature reserve on the North Norfolk coast.

Eminent conservationist Sydney Long helped to safeguard Scolt Head Island in 1922 and he then turned his attention to Cley Marsh. It already had a prominent reputation dating from the 1800s due to the collectors, gentlemen gunners and wildfowlers and became even more noteworthy in 1921 following a flood which left brackish pools, a fast growing reed bed and plenty of birds. The following year a ruff's nest was found (a species that had last nested in Norfolk in 1907 and has not nested in North Norfolk since). Not only was Long able to purchase the marsh in 1926 through the help of several financial backers, he also instigated the creation of the Norfolk Naturalist's Trust (now known as The Norfolk Wildlife Trust) in order to own and manage the site. Through his keen sense of foresight and with the efforts of three generations of the Bishop family as wardens, it has become a truly vital wildlife refuge.

Cley remains the Trust's flagship reserve despite the constant threat of flooding (which occurred again in 1953, 1978, 1996 and 2007) and has managed to attract a wonderful array of birdlife. With shooting outlawed in 1964, Cley became the ultimate sanctuary. Wader and wildfowl numbers began to soar through the autumn and winter months. The first bittern's nest was found in 1937, while black-tailed godwits nested for the first time in 1964. Cley along with neighbouring Salthouse had been the stronghold of avocets prior to their local extinction and it seems rather fitting that their present day status of relative 'abundance' should have grown from a recolonizing population that first reappeared and nested there in 1977. Add to this the growing number of rare vagrant species such as little whimbrel, rock and white-crowned sparrows, Pacific swift, slender-billed and Ross's gulls and red-necked stint that have all brought huge numbers of visitors flocking to Cley and there is little wonder that it has earned the title of 'Mecca for birdwatchers'

Further west from Cley and Holkham is Titchwell RSPB Reserve. It too had been reclaimed from the sea and farmed for generations only to be swamped with sea water following that violent night in 1953. The potential displayed by nesting little terns and Montagu's harriers and large flocks of wintering waders was enough to interest the RSPB who bought the 166 hectare marsh in 1973. Since then a great deal of effort and money has been put into creating the varied wetland that we see today. Hides and a lavish visitor's centre have ensured that every year tens of thousands of birdwatchers flock to the site, officially making it the most visited of the RSPB's reserves. Thanks to the work instigated by original warden Norman Sills, the reserve boasts a mixture of reed beds, open fresh water, brackish pools, fenland type meadows and mixed, damp woodland all alongside the original salt marsh that stretches to the east and west.

The region's first breeding marsh harriers nested at Titchwell in 1980, the same year as bitterns, and was soon followed by avocets. Alongside the growing numbers of waders and wildfowl its attractiveness for luring in many birds on passage migration has led to a fantastic list of rarities. It was enough, in fact, for Titchwell to rival Cley and officially become the most popular place in Britain for birdwatching.

The spring is as good a time as any to enjoy the area's wetland specialities. One bird that epitomises not only the spring but also the value of wetlands is the lapwing, formerly known locally as the 'green plover' and 'peeweep' alongside its other country wide name, the 'peewit'. All these names sum up this beautiful wader pretty well; its bottle green colouration, its unique vocalisations and its slow flapping display flight.

In the winter, lapwings are widespread on the area's farmland fields but by February and March the flocks start to become restless. Depending on the severity of the weather, wintering birds from different parts of the species European range may be present. Our own birds may remain locally or perhaps move to France, Spain or even west into Ireland. Then eastern European and Scandinavian birds replace them. As the flocks depart and our own birds return to their traditional marshland haunts, so it is a sure sign spring has arrived. For the cock lapwing it is a time to stake his territory; his distinctive highflying song flight always embodying the joys of spring. As he shouts out his plaintive and ringing calls he seems to be filled with a determined and enthusiastic fervour that nothing can prevent. His mission is to attract a mate and deter any other would be rival male lapwings and all around there are many

Titchwell Marsh, an RSPB reserve since 1973.

A flock of lapwings migrating over the North Norfolk coast.

more doing the same, rising into the sky to sing, to twist, tumble and cascade back to earth with their broad wings, flapping like a cloak in the wind.

Once they have paired and eggs are laid, he seldom leaves his mate's side, apart from the odd burst of aerial display and sometimes even further copulations with other females that may venture into his domain. Either way, after about three and a half weeks of incubation, the first delightful bundles of ungainly looking chicks emerge from their nests in late April. Although able to feed themselves they still need their parents for warmth and protection from weather and predators. Grey herons, carrion crows, sparrowhawks, kestrels, foxes and stoats all pose a threat and are vigorously mobbed if they come anywhere near the nesting fields. Such panicked attacks are usually just a means of confusing and seeing off potential threats and are usually carried out by more than just one species. If there are lapwings there are invariably redshanks and avocets too.

A rather more secretive bird of the marshes is the snipe. It prefers the partially hidden muddy margins of pools where mud, grass, rush and sedge come together, where it can probe undisturbed for worms, with its long, extremely sensitive bill. In the tangled world of a dyke or pool edge where fallen vegetation merges with varying shades of mud, the snipe's wonderfully, cryptic plumage often makes it invisible to the inexperienced watcher. For those who spend time in the hides at Cley, Titchwell or Holme then there is a far greater opportunity to actually watch a snipe feeding, particularly in the autumn months when many migrant birds arrive from the continent.

Unfortunately the snipe has long been in decline in Norfolk. The days when over 300 were shot during a cold snap at Holkham (back in 1859) are very much in the past, as is the time when even the smallest rough, damp patch of uncultivated land would attract breeding snipe. Since the 1800s when many wetlands were drained ever more snipe country has been lost and the modern day decline is rather more worrying as it is occurring in places that still appear suitable to the species needs. In modern times North Norfolk's breeding population has dropped from 44 displaying males in 1992 to only nine in 2007.

For a species that is generally so secretive, the snipe has a particularly showy display flight carried out in the spring and early summer that at least indicates whether any potential breeding birds are present. Not only is it fond of perching on fence posts where it utters a rhythmical, echoing call; it also frequently carries out its 'drumming' flight. The snipe rises high above his territory, before plummeting down like a stone. All the while a most peculiar, soft droning noise can be heard; this is its 'drumming', caused by the air rushing through its outer two tail feathers that are splayed out as it descends. As he almost comes to the ground, he might lift again for a repeat performance or simply stall his flight and alight amidst a series of high speed twisting, turning manoeuvres.

While the snipe was once a common bird and now in decline, the avocet is a bird whose fortunes have improved in recent years. The days when the 'clinkers' (as avocets were once known locally – a reference to their noisy call notes) were indiscriminately shot and driven to local extinction, are long in the past. For a long while it seemed that the avocet would be confined to the history books since its last nesting records at Salthouse were between 1822 and 1825. A false hope arose in 1941 when a pair tried to breed but failed. The much anticipated recolonisation finally took place in 1977 at Cley when four pairs raised six young between them. Since then this most elegant wader has gone from strength to strength. Just four years later, Cley boasted 26 pairs increasing to over 80 pairs by 1988. Other sites were soon to host them too. Returning to the old stronghold of Salthouse in 1981, they then graced Holme from 1982, Titchwell in 1984, Burnham Norton in 1989, Holkham in 1990 and Stiffkey in 1997. With somewhere in the region of 300 pairs now nesting annually along the North Norfolk coast it seems the avocet is now once more well and truly established.

The snipe is hanging on as a breeding bird in North Norfolk in very small numbers.

A courting pair of avocets, the prelude to mating.

Avocets are always interesting to watch, due to their very striking plumage and the distinctive method by which they feed, sweeping their delicate upturned bills from side to side through the water filtering out any potential prey item. They also have a very quaint, drawn out courtship ritual and it is not uncommon to see a male seemingly take an eternity to preen itself whilst his mate stands close by in a bent submissive pose. This is the prelude to mating and ultimately nesting.

The nest is usually just a scraped out hollow (sometimes lined with twigs, pebbles or shells if they can be found in the immediate vicinity) on an exposed island in the middle or at the edge of a pool and often very close to others of its kind. These colonies are ideal for avocets when incubating or rearing their young as the protection and alarm raising capabilities are greater than a lone pair could ever achieve. When breeding, avocets are exceptionally protective and will drive away anything perceived as a threat. They frequently chase away any other wader that ventures too close and often the whole colony will erupt in frenzy if a grey heron, carrion crow or marsh harrier flies over. Despite such dedicated parenthood, avocets can still face a number of setbacks. Pools that hold sufficient water early in the spring often dry out before the eggs hatch thus depriving the birds of food and leaving them more exposed to predation. This ultimately is the biggest problem, for both eggs and young and sometimes a whole colony can be wiped out overnight if a fox is active nearby, whilst grey herons have exhibited similar behaviour ravenously devouring eggs and young alike. Even coots have been seen smashing up the eggs of an entire colony at Titchwell. Whilst avocets have always been regarded as coastal birds, a few pairs have been found in more recent years spreading inland, some nesting alongside farm irrigation reservoirs and others in a potato field.

The black-tailed godwit is another wader that appears in good numbers. It, like the avocet, was once a common breeder in Norfolk's wetlands until it was persecuted to local extinction in the 19th century. It began to re-establish itself in small numbers in the fens during the 1930s eventually to be followed in the 1960s by several nesting attempts at Cley. Unfortunately bad weather and the constant attention of various predators ensured that out of several nesting attempts between 1964 and 1980, young were only fledged in 1973 and 1978. Elsewhere along the coast a pair nested at Holkham in 1990, only for the eggs to be taken by a fox.

While black-tailed godwits breed in damp lowland meadows right across Europe into Russia it is birds of the darker Icelandic race that now occur in North Norfolk in far greater numbers. These spend the winter in the estuaries of Britain, Iberia and Morocco and nest on the tundra and moorland of Iceland. Consequently many pass through our coastal marshes and since the mid 1990s increasing numbers not only winter, but also remain throughout the summer months. A flock of 300 on the wader scrapes at Titchwell and Cley or the meadows at Holkham is now quite a regular sight.

North Norfolk has long had the reputation of attracting impressive numbers of waders and the coastal grazing marshes are just as favoured as the mud flats, salt marshes and harbours, albeit to a different selection of species. The scrapes and pools at Cley and more recently Titchwell and Holkham provide wonderful opportunities for observing migrant waders as they pass north in the spring to their breeding grounds in the arctic tundra and then south again in the autumn to wintering grounds in Africa.

In the spring most of the birds are impatient and usually stop for shorter periods than in the autumn and are also fewer in numbers. Catch them in April and May, however and most will be showing their fine breeding plumage. The godwits are usually at their best then, as are greenshanks, spotted redshanks, wood sandpipers, Temminck's stints, dunlins, curlew sandpipers and ruff that all pass through in varying numbers.

In July, August and September the ruff becomes a common sight on our fresh water marshes, flocks frequently reaching three figures in a good year at Titchwell. The males, upon their return, will possess a magnificent head dress mixture of black, chestnut or white (their feather 'ruff') although this disappears fast as the birds soon start to moult.

Between 1964 and 1990, black-tailed godwits nested in small numbers on the coast.

A spotted redshank beginning to moult from its black breeding plumage.

By then yet more cosmopolitan travellers are also appearing. Autumn waders are usually easier to observe than in the spring as they seem less anxious and often stay for longer and appear in greater numbers. Spotted redshanks in their immaculate black breeding dress are usually the first birds to return in late June. The first of these Scandinavian breeders are females; having laid their eggs, they leave incubation and fledging duties solely to the males. Another June arrival is the green sandpiper, which is exclusively a lover of fresh water pools. It can be found anywhere during its migration from small farm ponds, even temporary pools and puddles, to lakesides, rivers, gravel pits and the fresh water lagoons of the coastal marshes. With very dark upperparts that contrast strongly with its white rump, the green sandpiper has a slight resemblance to a house martin in flight, hence its old country name; the 'martin snipe'.

Into late August and September most of the returning waders are pristine looking youngsters undertaking their first migration. Invariably there will be tiny little stints scurrying about on the mud, their immaculate back stripes the tell tale signs of fresh plumaged juveniles newly arrived from nests way off in northern Russia. Some years are better than others and in a good year uncharacteristically tame groups may appear on even the smallest of puddles along the coast. Again flocks numbering three figures have occurred. Never far away from little stints are curlew sandpipers. These waders are travellers of vast distances, breeding in the high arctic of Siberia and wintering in West Africa. While most adults in their brick red summer finery migrate in the spring from Africa across the Mediterranean, the autumn passage is more likely to bring them closer to our shores and if a good breeding season has occurred, large numbers of fine grey scaly plumaged youngsters descend to our marshes.

As with migrant passerines, there is also a very good chance of encountering a rare wader and North Norfolk's list is one of the finest from any area of the country. North American species such as Wilson's phalarope, American golden plover, killdeer, lesser yellowlegs, long-billed dowitcher and semi-palmated, buff-breasted, spotted, white-rumped, Baird's, solitary and pectoral sandpipers have all been recorded. From the Mediterranean to all points east as far off as eastern Siberia, come greater sandplover, marsh, terek, and broad-billed sandpipers, little whimbrel, oriental, collared and black-winged pratincoles, Pacific golden plover and red-necked stint. This is an impressive collection for any British county, yet all the more notable as they have all been recorded around Cley.

There is another wader that in recent years became part of the North Norfolk story, though despite one being shot at Blakeney way back in 1851 it has still to grace Cley reserve with an appearance. The black-winged stilt usually has a habit of dropping in further to the west, with the pools at Holme and Titchwell having the greater share of the sightings. Since one was seen at Holme in 1965, North Norfolk has only recorded a further seven individuals yet strangely enough the area currently has the greatest history of the species in all of Britain.

The black-winged stilt is found throughout much of the world's warmer regions across the United States, the Mediterranean, Africa and India, but it generally breeds no closer to the UK than Spain and France.

In 1987 Britain enjoyed an exceptional influx of black-winged stilts with up to 38 different individuals dotted around the country during a spell of exceptionally warm weather on the continent. Events culminated with a pair taking up residence and eventually nesting in the pools at Holme. With past breeding attempts confined to Nottinghamshire in 1945 and Cambridgeshire in 1983 this unprecedented episode proved to be one of the most exciting (and profitable) periods in the history of Holme reserve. Fortunately for both the staff of the reserve and the public, the hides that overlooked the pools enabled a constant 24 hour guard to occur and at the same time offered remarkable viewing opportunities to the thousands of visitors who flocked to witness the day to day routines of these elegant birds. Once nesting was underway the two stilts proved to be just as protective and aggressive as avocets in seeing off any would be threats to their eggs and the youngsters once they had hatched. Their efforts were

A juvenile little stint.

Titchwell's famous black-winged stilt.

rewarded with two chicks managing to fledge. It was also quite remarkable that upon finally deserting our coast in the August, the youngsters were seen a day later over 200 km away in Staffordshire.

Not surprisingly none of the stilts reappeared the following year and it seemed that North Norfolk's attractiveness to the species would once more revert to being only a temporary residence for any future overshooting migrants. It was not long, however, before the species once more unexpectedly made headlines in the region. In August 1993, following a journey that began in Northumberland and ended in the marshes of North Norfolk, a lone male black-winged stilt began what was subsequently the lengthiest stay ever by one of its kind in Britain. It favoured the brackish lagoons of Titchwell but occasionally wandered along to the beaches and tidal channels of Brancaster and Scolt Head. Normally a lone feeder, it sometimes roosted on the shore in the company of oystercatchers and bar-tailed godwits, while in the spring it even showed amorous behaviour towards the occasional female oystercatcher that ventured too close! Unfortunately it never did attract a mate and it was last seen in May 2005.

Another exotic bird that appears more frequently than in the past is the spoonbill. This large white heron-like bird gets its name from its long spoon shaped beak. When it feeds, the large spatulate bill tip is ploughed through the water to filter fish and invertebrates from beneath the surface. Sometimes in a rich feeding area, two or three birds may be seen together, heads down feeding with almost synchronised sweeps through the water. Such encounters always remain memorable as most feeding is carried out at dusk or in darkness and for many observers all they often see of a spoonbill is a motionless white shape, head and bill tucked under its wing, fast asleep.

Occasionally spoonbills bearing colour rings appear in mid summer along the coast. This bird was ringed as a nestling in Holland in May 2004 and appeared at Cley between June and August 2008.

A successful catch by a spoonbill.

Spoonbills nest regularly across the North Sea in Holland in loosely formed marsh side colonies. Birds that have overshot their destination during the spring migration often drop in to our marshes for a week or two, while mid summer appearances are often birds that have failed in their own breeding attempts or are immatures not yet able to compete within a competitive nesting colony. Such information is known as the appearance of birds bearing individual colour rings have been detected along the coast on more than one occasion. Sometimes the odd bird even winters, preferring then to feed in the larger salt marsh creeks and channels. A winter sighting these days does not seem so unusual as it once would have due to all the little egrets about, but in days gone by they were deemed very unusual and due to the collectors and gunners, most ended up shot. Even the nesting colonies that could once be found in the Norfolk broads (up until the seventeenth century) faced the same level of persecution and ultimately suffered the same fate as many of the County's other lost marsh birds.

Currently hopes are high that it will not be long before successful breeding occurs in Norfolk and as spoonbills are now pretty much a regular spring and summer visitor to the region's marshes, surely there could be no finer place. Flocks of up to 17 have summered, regularly commuting between three main sites, Cley, Holkham and Titchwell.

Pinkfeet geese alighting on an autumn stubble field near Burnham Market.

Chapter Six

A winter of wildfowl

When the excitement of the summer's breeding season has long gone and the autumn wader passage draws to its close, the coastal grazing marshes of North Norfolk are visited by another cosmopolitan gathering of travellers. Late autumn welcomes fantastic numbers of wildfowl; ducks and geese that are moving south from the hostilities of a northern winter. Unlike most of the waders mentioned in the last chapter, the wildfowl arrive to actually spend the winter here as opposed to passing through to destinations further south.

For wintering ducks, the combination of salt marsh and fresh water grazing meadows side by side is an ideal mix of habitats. Whilst breeding species such as mallard, pochard, shoveler and tufted ducks have their numbers augmented in the winter by continental migrants there are three other species, which are almost solely winter visitors or passage migrants. Teal, pintail and wigeon all arrive in the autumn months to exploit the winter-feeding opportunities offered on the coast.

Among the first to return are the teal. These small dabbling ducks with their high pitched squeaking calls are beautifully marked birds, particularly the drake with his chestnut head, set off with an iridescent green flash behind its eyes that is framed in a delicate yellow border. Very small numbers have nested occasionally at Cley, Burnham Norton and Holkham but such occurrences are rare. Unlike the other ducks there is always a distinct arrival in June and July of teal. Whether these are failed or non breeders is still not known or indeed from where they originate. By August and September, numbers increase further and there are often flocks of a substantial size present. As the autumn moves on, good numbers of newly arriving migrants from central Europe, Russia and Scandinavia pass offshore during northerly and easterly winds, many alighting on the pools of our coastal marshes.

Whilst the teal is the smallest of our wintering ducks, the pintail is one of the largest and a drake is arguably one of the most spectacular looking. Its characteristic long neck and tail gives it great elegance, unmatched by its companions on the marsh and heightened further by its subtle chocolate and white head and neck markings, its vermiculated grey body and creamy flank patches. Wintering birds arrive from western Siberia as well as Iceland, Scandinavia and the Baltic states. Late September into October sees the peak of overhead and offshore migration along the coast and by November and December, flocks of several hundred will be present in the Cley and Blakeney area.

A pintail's long neck enables it to stretch down below the surface of the water and feed on all manner of aquatic vegetation that other dabbling ducks struggle to reach. Those feeding on the saltings, seek out the same tiny *hydrobia* snails that shelducks love. The flocks freely move between Blakeney Harbour and the reserve at Cley, where a peak of 1519 birds was reached in December 1997. Similar habitat around Brancaster and Scolt Head is also utilised with Titchwell used like Cley as a loafing area. The Holkham area is less favoured although occasionally flocks of up to 85 have gathered in the early winter, joining up with the newly arrived pinkfeet geese to feed on barley stubble up to a few miles inland.

The one species of duck that really is deeply associated with North Norfolk's marshes is the wigeon. It arrives here to winter in numbers that easily surpass those of any other species of duck that frequent the coast. At one time it was a species that was found more on the salt marshes than anywhere else, the beds of eel grass (which many locals even called 'wigeon grass') being their favoured food. Wigeon consequently became a favourite quarry of local

A group of drake teal.

A drake pintail pictured in a heavy shower.

wildfowlers but since the widespread decline of eel grass the wigeon switched more to grazing on the protected meadowland of the coastal nature reserves. Since the late 1980s the wet, well-grazed fields between Burnham Norton and Holkham have become the site that now regularly attracts the largest numbers. January 2002 provided one of the biggest concentrations of recent years when over 19,000 were counted along the whole coast from which total Holkham NNR had a record of over 14,000. Similar habitat at Holme, Blakeney, Stiffkey and Cley offers just as good viewing opportunities, although involving lesser numbers.

Such spectacular flocks are short in their stay and by March most will be departing for their breeding grounds in Iceland, Scandinavia and Russia. Sadly there are always a few that are forced to stay, victims of a bad shot from a wildfowler. It is always a sad sight to see a bird as fine as a drake wigeon or pintail wandering helpless across the marshes, immaculate in its plumage but handicapped due to a badly wounded wing or limping foot. For it, the marshes of North Norfolk will be its final resting place, no breeding season in a lush Icelandic lakeside, only a slow death, unless that is, a hungry fox gets to it first.

Another species that winters here in huge numbers is the pink-footed goose. Norfolk is a winter home to a third of and sometimes perhaps almost half the world population and the marshes and fields of the north coast probably have a greater affinity with the species than anywhere else in the country.

In chapter three, the habit of roosting on the foreshore by the pinkfeet was discussed, as was their attractiveness to the wildfowlers of the coast. Fortunately some early conservationists (many of whom also shot) had the courage and will to see certain areas made into protected sanctuaries for the geese. Here the birds could rest and feed in peace, free from the constant barrage of shots that they faced at dusk and dawn as they flew between night time roosts and daytime feeding areas. Foremost amongst these conservationists was the Earl of Leicester at

Above: The most abundant of the ducks seen on the North Norfolk coast in winter is the wigeon.

Below: Courting wigeon can frequently be seen, yet it is usually only the sick and wounded that summer.

Holkham who at the end of the nineteenth century allowed the pinkfeet to graze and sleep on his coastal meadows without the disturbance they received elsewhere. By doing so he began a long association between place and species that has gone on to this day. In fact, for a species that was originally identified in Norfolk at Holkham in 1841, its movements and habits have changed very little since, even if its population has grown to numbers that an early concerned Earl could not have foreseen. Between those early days of wildlife protection and the enormous numbers that occur today, there was a lean spell where numbers dropped until the species all but abandoned the area.

With the advent of the Second World War, the marshes of Stiffkey and Warham were the site of a military firing zone and the sound of large anti-aircraft guns near Wells provided constant disturbance. This, combined with the conversion of Holkham's meadows to cultivated fields, left nowhere for the geese to roost or rest in peace. Instead they chose the solace of the Wash and it was not until the late 1970s that the first birds began to return to Holkham. Most stays were only brief and regular wintering did not take place again until 1980. Since then numbers along the coast have increased at an amazing rate, by the early 1990s, a high of over 68,000 was attained in January 1994, increasing steadily thereafter to over 100,000 between 2003 and 2007.

The first pinkfeet begin to appear in September with the middle of the month being the traditional time for their arrival. In recent years this date has progressively become earlier, with 3rd September the earliest date. Invariably the first party returns to Holkham, dropping in from the west. Once they have arrived it is not long before more small groups follow the same flight line day after day. Nowadays by the end of September it is possible to see well over 2000 birds congregated on the fields at Holkham, setting the scene for even more as October turns to November. The habits of the returning hordes are basically centred solely at Holkham when they first arrive. Here they spend most of their time, sleeping, preening, washing in the fresh water pools and grazing on the meadow grass. In September the sugar beet that they have come

The marshes at Holkham have traditionally been a place of sanctuary for wintering pinkfeet.

to depend on is still deep in the ground and the geese choose to either stay at Holkham or move inland to stubble fields where they can feed from fresh emerging grasses and spilt grain. Early on in the season they do not venture far, in fact always staying close enough so that when disturbed they can soon return to the meadows at Holkham; exactly the same behaviour as in the 1800s when in addition to stubble, fields of ley grass were grazed.

Since the new millennium the safety that Holkham has provided has also extended to the site becoming an additional roosting site; the extensive fresh water pools offering a suitable alternative to the foreshore at Warham that is still stalked at dusk and dawn by a smaller yet just as dedicated number of wildfowlers than in the past. At first the Holkham pools were only used in this way in the autumn until the sugar beet harvest got underway, but by the winter of 2004/05 the geese were still returning to them at dusk even during mid winter.

When the sugar beet harvest does get into full swing in November, the peak numbers of geese are present. They time their movements from other parts of Britain such as at Martin Mere in Lancashire and eastern Scotland so that they are in Norfolk before Christmas to feed on the leaves and root 'tops' of sugar beet which are discarded on the fields during the mechanical harvesting of the crop. This usually means that less time is spent at Holkham during the daytime, although they always make a touchdown there if they are disturbed, coming even from considerable distances inland. During the bright nights that a full moon guarantees, the geese change their habits and switch from day feeding to night feeding. Consequently there may be a very large congregation (possibly all of North Norfolk's birds) roosting during the day at Holkham.

Pinkfeet numbers peak either just before Christmas or into the New Year. By late January into February numbers start to dwindle and a month later the vast bulk will have gone. For those that do remain, the sugar beet harvest is all but over and there is no rich larder of 'tops' left to exploit. Once more they resort to the Holkham marshes. This can be a good time to observe their daily routines at close quarters as they seem more tolerant and contented than

The large rolling fields of North Norfolk after the sugar beet has been harvested offer the pinkfeet some of the richest feeding in the British Isles.

Pinkfeet remain in their families within the large flocks and often squabble with rivals over food.

when feeding inland. Whilst the geese have grown to be quite trusting of people at Lady Anne's Drive (a favoured spot), due to the constant comings and goings of cars, anywhere else and they are always wary and fit to fly. Low flying aircraft can trigger such a reaction as will a grey heron or a even a confused hare that might run into a flock, seemingly scaring itself just as much as the geese around it. Raptors such as harriers are usually ignored although flocks sometimes depart at the appearance of a peregrine. Whilst a pinkfoot might seem too large a prey item for a peregrine, an occasional kill does occur. At Holkham a large female was once watched plucking a dead pinkfoot, while at Holme in 2003 one lucky observer actually witnessed a peregrine kill a pinkfoot. It stooped, striking the poor goose twice in the neck before it fell to the ground.

With the last migrants gone by early May it is then only the sick and wounded that are left to end their days, usually as summer fox victims. One pair of pinkfeet which stayed at Stiffkey in 1999 nested in a clump of nettles in the meadows alongside the river. Unfortunately, despite 11 eggs escaping predation, they proved infertile and failed to hatch. Unsurprisingly this remains Norfolk's only breeding record.

For many people a lone pinkfoot is a rather drab goose, no more exciting than a feral greylag. The great beauty and character of pinkfeet becomes apparent when they are seen in dense, noisy flocks. There is another species of goose, however, that regularly spends the winter here, which is without question far more beautiful when encountered at close quarters. It is the white-fronted goose. Not only does it possess the combination of a pink bill contrasting with vivid orange legs, but its typical 'grey goose' plumage is also enlivened with a broad white band between bill and eyes and almost velvet black belly bars. These latter two features are the marks of mature adults; the youngsters lack evidence of either until they are approaching the end of their first year.

The 'white-fronts' arrival date seems far less predictable than the pinkfeet; perhaps conditions elsewhere dictate their migration. It is known through ringing recoveries that Britain's

*White-fronted geese arrive annually from northern Russia in the winter
to the grazing marshes at Holkham.*

wintering birds originate from breeding grounds along the White Sea coast of northern Russia and that they pass through the Baltic States and Denmark on their south westerly journey to Belgium, Holland and England. Presumably if they find good undisturbed feeding *en route* they will prolong their stop. They also come to North Norfolk in far fewer numbers than pinkfeet with normally only 300 to 400 by the time they reach their annual peak. Generally the first families begin to appear in November, sometimes late October, but usually the bulk of birds do not appear until late December or even early January. Numbers often increase with mid winter influxes of birds from Holland, particularly if the weather there becomes more severe.

The one thing that is certain about the white-fronts is where they will appear. Like the first returning pinkfeet, they too make their initial touch down in the Holkham area. Unlike the pinkfeet, however, which after a while begin to travel widely within the county to feed, the white-fronts settle for a winter nibbling at the grass on the grazing marshes at Holkham. Their time here is short and by mid March they will be gone, leaving our familiar coastal marshes behind, for the more desolate tundra and northern shores of Russia.

Whilst the pinkfeet, white-fronts and brent are the most conspicuous and commonly encountered wild geese found during a North Norfolk winter, there are other species that appear infrequently or in lesser numbers. The most regular of these are barnacle and bean geese. Each year a few barnacles appear amongst the pinkfeet indicating that like their companions they have originated from Greenland nesting grounds. Occasionally some also arrive during stormy weather in October and these are usually birds that are heading from Svalbard in the Arctic Ocean to their traditional wintering grounds in the Solway Firth area of southern Scotland. By far the largest groups (a flock of 155 appeared in January 1984) have occurred when extremely hard weather has forced Dutch wintering birds off the continent across the

North Sea to Norfolk. These birds are from nesting grounds further east in the Russian islands of Novaya Zemlya. Unfortunately the presence of escaped birds from wildfowl collections can cloud the appearance of genuinely wild birds and feral populations have become established in the south of Norfolk and in Suffolk. Even here in North Norfolk, a pair nested at Holkham Lake for the first time in 2004, and by 2008 two pairs were breeding. It is possible that in the future, barnacle geese will become more widespread, feral residents.

A pair of barnacle geese, freshly arrived in a mid winter cold snap,
make the most of feeding from sugar beet tops.

Bean geese are very similar to pinkfeet except they show orange legs and bill markings. They too have several distinct geographical populations that extend east across Europe into much of northern Asia and the form most likely to be encountered here is the tundra bean goose. It has an orange-banded bill and nests on the tundra and river deltas of Russia. These birds normally winter in Holland although small numbers (usually less than 20) arrive annually in mid winter and join up with either the pinkfeet or whitefronts. Whilst the latter generally avoid flying inland to feed on fields of sugar beet tops, bean geese soon follow the example of the pinkfeet.

Just like the appearance of rare migrating vagrant waders in Norfolk, the arrival of a rare goose amidst the vast numbers of commoner species has now become something to be expected each year. Nothing can be guaranteed, but species with decidedly North American/Greenland origins such as Greenland white-fronted, lesser Canada, snow and Ross's geese have all appeared amongst the pinkfeet. Likewise, from Eurasian stock, lesser white-fronted geese have turned up amongst the white-fronts and red-breasted geese and black brants sometimes arrive with the brent geese. Some observers are content to dismiss such birds as escapees, yet considering the huge numbers of wild geese that now arrive in North Norfolk and the undeniable migratory capabilities of such birds, there is every chance that most are indeed genuine wild birds.

Above: Small numbers of other geese appear amongst the pinkfeet.
This juvenile Ross's goose was near Wighton in January 2002.

Below: Between 1983 and 2007 up to eight red-breasted geese have been seen in North Norfolk
including this pair at Wells in March 2007 amongst brent geese.

A sedge warbler sings out loud from a reed stem at Cley.

Chapter Seven

Secrets of a hidden world

As we have seen in the previous chapters, the grazing marshes and fresh water pools are home to important numbers of wetland birds, yet the reed beds that grow harmoniously nearby, attract equally interesting wildlife.

A reed bed is a transitional environment, the intermediate world between open water and damp scrubland. In the margins of wetlands reeds are able to flourish but as they age the understorey becomes littered with dead and decaying stems. As these dry out invasive scrub plants begin to take root and without a suitable depth of water or controlled management, the transformation from reeds to fledgling woodland will soon begin. In years gone by, when there was great need for thatching materials, there was a benefit in maintaining reed beds. Unfortunately throughout the twentieth century there was a decreasing demand and many reed beds fell into a state of decline. This, combined with a push for drainage and land reclamation, meant that Britain lost up to half of its reed beds.

In North Norfolk the reclaimed grazing marshes and brackish lagoons have ensured that there is enough suitable habitat for reeds to thrive and attract a small population of the creatures that help to give this environment such a unique character. Titchwell and Cley have substantial reed beds and at Cley in particular (along with nearby Salthouse) there is still regular harvesting carried out during the winter months. Smaller yet equally as important reed beds can be found at Blakeney, Burnham Overy, Burnham Norton, Brancaster and Holme. Even places with no substantial reed beds can boast plenty of their occupants due to the reed edged dykes that

The reed bed beside the East Bank at Cley, a famous birdwatching site.

create field boundaries. The flood plain meadows beside the River Stiffkey are amongst the more recent sites in a countrywide initiative where conservation work is in the process of creating brand new reed beds to attract more of the species that have been in decline.

A reed bed might seem like an impenetrable swamp but take time to watch over one and its secrets begin to be revealed. During the summer there are usually plenty of dragonflies that add distinctive splashes of colour to the channels of open water. North Norfolk may not be able to attract as many species as some Broadland or Fenland areas yet those that do occur, prosper. The large red, azure, blue-tailed and common blue damselflies are among the first to emerge in the spring and early summer, swiftly followed by the broad-bodied and four-spotted chasers, black-tailed skimmers, common and ruddy darters, southern and migrant hawkers and the emperor dragonfly. Other species have also begun to appear. Yellow-winged darters from the continent arrived in above average numbers all along the coast in 1995 and 2006, lesser emperor from southern Europe was seen at Titchwell in 2003 and ever growing numbers of the small red-eyed damselfly, a species that appeared in Britain for the first time in 1999, has colonized several sites along the coast. Without doubt one of the most impressive of the newcomers is the banded demoiselle. Despite being a common species on rivers and canals throughout much of southern and western Britain; it was seldom recorded in North Norfolk. However, in the late 1990s it began to move up the rivers to the coast where it is now an established resident, although a thinly scattered one. On warm August days small red-eyed damselflies, yellow-winged darters and banded demoiselles are even noted arriving in from the sea landing in the marram grass of the dunes and the suaeda of the adjacent salt marshes.

The reed-filled dykes and channels are also home to a small number of mammals. Otters are glimpsed very occasionally. A small population has slowly grown since the 1990s when a reintroduction scheme in East Anglia successfully re-established them following virtual local

The four-spotted chaser is a common species.
in the north coast marshes.

One of the newest species to colonize North
Norfolk is the small red-eyed damselfly.

Below: The banded demoiselle is common along rivers and in recent years has spread out onto some of the North Norfolk marshes.

extinction in the mid 1980s. With spraints and tracks occasionally found on both the Glaven and Stiffkey rivers as well as on the marshes it seems the future is now much brighter for a species once seriously threatened with eradication by a combination of hunting and pollution.

Another species that seems to be in a similar predicament at present yet can still be seen more easily than an otter is the water vole. The water vole was once a familiar sight in most English waterways yet it has become increasingly scarce. Between 1990 and 1998 it was estimated that its population had dropped by 88% making it the fastest declining British mammal. These were grim statistics for a creature that was once widespread and common. Pollution and fragmented populations were two of the problems while the spread of escaped North American mink, one of the most voracious predators of the waterway, only added to its plight.

Despite such problems water voles can still be encountered at Cley, Holkham and Titchwell although in fewer numbers than before. If fortunate, they may be seen out of the water sitting on their haunches nibbling a piece of vegetation that is gripped tightly with their front feet. When disturbed, water voles are swift to jump into the water with a distinctive plop. They either dive underwater with a trail of bubbles being the only clue to their presence, or paddle off out of harms way. When swimming, water voles always have a distinctive look, with head and back held clear of the surface.

The water vole is still present in small numbers in North Norfolk.

Another relatively new addition to the wildlife of North Norfolk is the Chinese water deer.

One mammal that has recently colonised the reed beds and marshes of North Norfolk is the Chinese water deer. Like the similar sized muntjac that is commonly encountered in our wooded parts, the Chinese water deer is an introduced species. Whereas muntjac are short legged and dumpy with an almost pig-like demeanour, Chinese water deer are more elegantly proportioned with the males showing sharp tusks (two elongated teeth) and they completely lack any antlers. Having first escaped from Whipsnade Zoo in 1929, they spread slowly throughout southern England, favouring damp woods, river valleys and reed beds. Although a thriving population has existed in the Norfolk Broads for quite some time it is only really since the new millennium that the species has become truly established in North Norfolk. Dawn and dusk offer the best viewing opportunities, with Holme, Holkham and Cley all hosting small numbers. Despite being an introduced species, numbers have declined so much in its North Korean and Chinese home land that it has been deemed as 'near threatened', making the UK's small but growing numbers (estimated at 10% of the world population) worth conserving.

While reed beds and their waterways are a haven for dragonflies and might provide the odd chance encounter with a water vole, it is the birds that provide the biggest draw for the enthusiastic naturalist. Not only are rare birds able to find a home there but so do many of our commoner species. Familiar ducks such as mallard, gadwall, tufted duck, shoveler and pochard and also little grebes are able to nest there. Coots and moorhens are never far away while another close relative, the water rail, also loves the safety a reed bed provides. Although it has a distinctive appearance it is only rarely glimpsed scuttling through the edge of the reeds; its shrill squeals are more likely to betray its presence. Water rails are also sometimes encountered out on the salt marshes, feeding in tiny creeks or underneath *suaeda* bushes.

The bittern is a bird that is truly the essence of the mysterious hidden world of the reed bed. Not only is it rare but also exceptionally secretive. Its appearance blends in so well with the

Above: The water rail sometimes ventures out from the depths of the reed bed.

Below: The bittern remains one of the most secretive of North Norfolk's birds.

reeds that it often seems invisible within seconds. In recent years it has provided the initiative for much conservation work. Choked up reed beds have been rejuvenated by intensive scrub clearance and many others have been created in the hope that one day they might attract a bittern.

The bittern is a shorter, stockier relative of the grey heron. It differs in a yellow brown plumage that is neatly patterned in jagged black feathers on its back and narrow stripes down its throat, neck and chest. Bitterns tend to live a solitary life, hidden away in the depths of the reeds where their cryptic plumage gives them perfect camouflage. This is never more evident than when a bittern is startled or when it periodically takes a break from feeding to scan its surroundings. Immediately it adopts an alert pose, with neck and bill stretched skyward. It can transform in a second from a squat shape huddled at the base of the reeds to a long narrow form almost as tall as the reeds themselves. Not only is its plumage so beautifully adapted but so too are its feet. At the end of its stout yellow-green legs are sets of long reptilian-like toes and claws that enable it to scurry about with ease through the soggy, matted understorey of a reed bed. Just as importantly they also allow the bittern to clamber up or along the stems of reeds.

Bitterns usually begin their breeding season preparations in the early spring when the male advertises his presence with a deep, resonating 'boom'. This unmistakable noise is often the only way bitterns can be detected but it has long been known that once mating has occurred he shows no further interest in any other aspect of nesting, or rearing offspring instead he prefers to continue booming and if possible mate again with another female.

If bitterns are breeding successfully, then, by June-July, the females will begin their feeding flights and this is often the most reliable time for a sighting. Bitterns feed on all manner of aquatic life from eels, fish, frogs and toads to freshwater shrimps, crayfish and even water shrews. If such prey cannot be found within the reed bed then they are forced to fly out to nearby ditches and fresh water ponds. Feeding grounds up to two miles from the nest have been recorded.

Most observers gain their first view of a bittern as it flies up from the reeds.

Wintertime also offers a rare chance for watching bitterns, with migrant birds arriving at coastal localities in October and November, sometimes settling into the smallest of reed edged pools. Some of these are likely to be wandering birds from elsewhere in East Anglia, while others are undoubtedly continental birds escaping cold conditions. Bitterns cannot survive prolonged hard winter weather and starvation in spells of severe, penetrating frosts has been the cause of many deaths.

Due to the usual culprits of hunting and habitat loss, the bittern became extinct in Britain by the middle of the nineteenth century and when a few birds attempted recolonizing they were instantly deemed as collectable. Despite persecution, the bittern did finally return as a breeder to the Norfolk Broads in 1911 and very slowly the population increased and expanded, although it was not until 1937, when a nest was found at Cley that the species was first recorded as breeding in North Norfolk. The large block of reeds (some 43 hectares) on the Norfolk Wildlife Trust's reserve at Cley has proved attractive for intermittent nesting ever since. British numbers reached a peak in the 1950s when up to 70-80 males were booming and by the 1980s five sites on our coast temporarily attracted breeding bitterns.

Sadly things started to go dreadfully wrong again and a nationwide population crash reached an all time low in 1997 when only 11 booming males were heard throughout Britain. At the start of the new millennium, Cley was the sole North Norfolk locality. Thankfully by 2004 the British population was back up to 55 booming males although in North Norfolk the birds were still only nesting at Cley. Since then another four sites along the coast have been reoccupied and in 2008 up to 75 boomers were spread throughout England, creating great optimism amongst those directly involved with their conservation.

To see a bittern actually swimming across open water is a very rare sight indeed.

A male marsh harrier hunting over the reeds at Cley.

Another reed bed specialist that like the bittern, was once ruthlessly persecuted yet was always thought of as being a Norfolk speciality, is the marsh harrier. Unlike the bittern it has had a rapid turn around in its fortunes and is currently enjoying a population boom.

Marsh harriers are large, long winged raptors that can feed on birds up to the size of a mallard. Smaller birds, however, particularly fledgling coots, moorhens, wildfowl and waders are all actively hunted in the breeding season. Mammals such as rats, voles and rabbits and even frogs, toads and birds eggs are just as likely to be taken.

Marsh harriers are currently at their highest recorded density in the region and there are few areas of reed bed or the damp scrubby margins of our coastal grazing marshes that have not hosted breeding birds at some stage. This was not always the case. Marsh harriers went from being relatively abundant predators of the Broads and Fens at the start of the nineteenth century to becoming extinct as British breeding bird by its end. It was rather fitting that a bird that was often known as the 'Norfolk hawk' should return to breed in the Norfolk Broads due to dedicated protection initially from a few sympathetic landowners. From being the county's rarest breeding bird, nesting sporadically from the early 1900s to the 1930s, it had progressed by 2001 to a total of over 100 known nests in Norfolk alone. Titchwell had the area's first breeding pair in 1980 and since then the north coast population increased to about 45 nesting females by 2007. With most breeding on nature reserves it seems their future is bright. Interestingly many are now nesting in autumn sown cereal and oil seed rape fields inland. Here breeding birds face the threat of agricultural machinery. Ever vigilant farm workers have succeeded in saving many a nest full of youngsters, although some certainly perish.

Small, but increasing numbers of marsh harriers are now wintering on the coast, unlike the majority which are summer migrants. They arrive from March onwards and usually remain well into September and October before heading south to Spain and Africa. The finest time to observe marsh harriers is in the spring when the male is at the height of his courtship rituals. And what a display he puts on! He will begin by gliding around his territory before gradually gaining height, often until he is a mere speck in the sky. He emphasizes his presence by constantly uttering a far crying, plaintive yelp. It is a note very similar to the beginning of a lapwing's call and can often be heard when the bird is so high it can barely be seen. He combines this call with his 'sky dance'; a performance of acrobatic flying that is one of the most spectacular displays given by any British bird. What begins with gentle undulations finishes with deep, fast swoops and sometimes complete somersaults, before dropping to the ground in a descent that looks as if he could be completely out of control. As he plummets there can be another couple of high speed upside down twists or turns, sometimes narrowly missing crashing into the ground below before finally stalling in the wind and gently landing with wings held out and legs outstretched. This ritual is not only intended to attract a mate but also to warn any other male looking for territory to stay away. Even when nest building is in progress, a settled male is often drawn up to sky dance if another potential rival appears overhead. The imminent lure of breeding is, of course, the main reason for such a display and the female often joins him high in the sky. Once the nest is made and eggs are laid, so the pair becomes rather more elusive. The male might well continue his display rituals as he often manages to attract a second and sometimes even third female with which he mates. Such polygamy is not unusual and in this instance when the young eventually hatch, the female will then hunt far and wide, rather than relying solely on her mate for prey.

By late June-early July the dark brown, almost black-looking juveniles make their first tentative flights. Their noisy hunger calls and their habit of perching on bush tops close to the nest site can make them most conspicuous. Fledglings can number from one to five and up until mid August they guarantee easy viewing as they are still dependant on their parents and often remain in the vicinity of the nest site.

At the other end of the size scale, there are a number of small birds that thrive in stands of reeds. In springtime, the reed beds come alive with the chattering songs of two species of

Spring is the time to see the spectacular interactions between a pair of marsh harriers.

After fledging, juvenile marsh harriers still rely on their parents for food.

warbler that arrive each April to proclaim their territories. Both reed and sedge warblers spend the winter months in sub Saharan Africa, but each year they return in good numbers to take advantage of an abundance of insect life that emerges from the surrounding vegetation. Whilst reed warblers tend to be rather elusive, only venturing on to the reed tops to sing when totally undisturbed, sedge warblers are rather bolder. Not only do they sing from exposed bush tops within reed beds but they also undertake a jerky song flight above their territory that ends in a parachuting-like descent to the reeds. Such behaviour makes them an easy bird to census and a total of up to 242 singing birds, found along the coast between Burnham Norton and Wells during the 2008 breeding season, give an indication of their relative abundance.

The real specialist passerine of the East Anglian reed beds, however, is the bearded tit, as it remains a rare breeding bird in the much of the British Isles. A national survey in 2002 recorded a maximum total of 559 pairs and while the Norfolk Broads remains a stronghold, in North Norfolk small numbers nest annually in the Blakeney-Cley-Salthouse area, Holkham NNR and Titchwell RSPB reserve.

The male bearded tit with its colourful plumage is without doubt one of Britain's most exotic-looking resident birds. In comparison the cinnamon coloured female is rather a plain looking bird, lacking the male's flamboyant head markings yet still sporting the same long tail and unique chinking call notes. These distinctive vocalizations are often the first indication that bearded tits are nearby, as they often remain hidden in the reeds where they feed at ground level. Here they shuffle along with tails half-cocked. Despite its small size, the bearded tit in Norfolk was more frequently referred to by the Victorian reed cutters and marsh men as the 'reed pheasant'.

Bearded tits thrive in warm summers when they are able to produce up to three broods. If the winter remains mild they can survive but during hard weather, when heavy snow falls cover the reed heads that provide their food, many will perish. As well as feeding around the reed cutters in the winter, birds at Brancaster and Titchwell are often seen feeding among the reeds that grow on the edge of the salt marshes. Here they are able to forage for the seeds of plants such as samphire, annual seablite and sea purslane.

For most of the year bearded tits can be rather elusive, but warm, still days in September and October (particularly after a successful breeding season) often provide wonderful viewing opportunities. Family parties group together to form even larger flocks until they gradually become more unsettled and restless. Brave noisy individuals adorn the tops of the reeds before finally launching themselves high into the sky. They then circle overhead before plummeting back deep into the reeds. Such behaviour can entice others to become braver and venture out. Groups may join from other areas of the reed bed and sometimes without warning they ascend *en masse* and after circling overhead might return or leave the area completely. These sudden, unpredictable movements are known as eruptions and result in bearded tits being recorded from unlikely places. Sometimes they pass along the coast at such a great height that they are only heard. Some observers along the coast have been fortunate enough to find bearded tits in the *suaeda* of Blakeney Point, in brambles and willows at Wells and in the gorse bushes of Stiffkey and Morston. Ringing evidence has confirmed that not only do our English birds move from site to site but we also receive continental arrivals.

The male bearded tit is one of the UK's most exotic-looking birds.

Kelling Heath is one of North Norfolk's finest heathland sites.

Chapter Eight

An ancient landscape

Most naturalists who visit North Norfolk are attracted first and foremost by the wonderful diversity of the coast. Yet those who limit their explorations to the sand dunes, mud flats and salt marshes will be missing out on a rural landscape, steeped in history and home to an equally fascinating variety of birds and animals. For those who feel that the coast is too overcrowded, particularly in the height of summer, then less hectic surroundings inland can provide an ideal alternative often only minutes away.

The most ancient of the inland habitats is without doubt heathland. Although North Norfolk does not boast a large acreage of this land form which has been disappearing over much of southern England for many years, it does have Salthouse and Kelling heaths. They are two relatively small yet fine examples and are situated in the east of the region sandwiched between the coast and Holt.

Both areas seem like relics from the past; tiny islands of heathland in an otherwise uniform landscape that has been constantly modified to meet changing agricultural practices. Yet before man was able to leave his mark on the land it was the forces of nature that carved out the shape of the countryside. Between the years 500,000 and 10,000 BC a series of Ice Ages cast their arctic grip on the British Isles and two of these covered the whole of Norfolk under a great depth of ice. The Wolstonian Glaciation arrived over 225,000 years ago and left the county as a frozen land of tundra for 100,000 years and it was during its final northerly retreat that much of North Norfolk's current landscape took its shape. The melting ice and receding glaciers deposited millions of tons of sand, gravel and stones ultimately forming the heaths at Kelling and Salthouse and the nearby 'downs' at Wiveton. Man eventually left his mark on the land and cleared away most of Britain's prehistoric forests yet it was found that heathland areas were too acidic for basic agriculture to be successful. Today the heaths often create a sense of timelessness where man has done little to alter this ancient link to the past. Yet in reality heaths were just as much a focus to man's progress and survival as was the surrounding farmland. Indeed it was his past actions, slashing and burning woodland, which in some instances created the heathland and then, by keeping it as open land he established an environment that had more in common with southern Europe.

Heaths in the past were commonly used as a place for grazing sheep and ponies, for rabbit warrens and for acquiring firewood from the gorse, while heather was used for thatching and bedding. Kelling Heath's importance can be dated back to the years between 6,500 and 3,500 BC with the earliest evidence of a settlement in the area. Similarly Salthouse Heath has ancient links to the past with the largest collection of Bronze Age burial mounds in Norfolk.

The reliance upon heaths began to wane throughout the nineteenth and twentieth centuries and without regular grazing or burning, many such places began to revert to birch and oak woodland. Other areas were put to the plough, built upon or were planted with conifers. As with many other parts of southern England, Norfolk subsequently lost much of its heathland, an estimated 90% over a 200 year period. Such statistics only heighten conservationists concerns for such a specialised habitat, where its natural inhabitants might be few in number, but are restricted in their range due to their reliance upon such places to survive. It is also very clear how important places like Salthouse and Kelling have become, where constant management is now a conservation necessity so they can remain a fitting reminder of times gone by.

Salthouse and Kelling Heaths are situated on high ground overlooking the coastal marshes and sea to their north. They are at their finest in the height of summer when the blooms of heather and gorse bring a glorious splash of colour to the land. The low growing heather comes in two species here; the more widespread true heather, which produces a beautiful swathe of purple in late summer and bell heather that flowers in July. Gorse is a common heathland plant that rapidly grows to impenetrable scrub if left unmanaged. In the past this was not a problem as 'furze' as it was known, was regularly cut and made into faggots to provide a hot burning fuel, particularly favoured for heating local bakers' ovens. Even the thorny vegetation had its uses, being pulled behind horses on cultivated land to provide a fine harrow-like implement. There are in fact two species of gorse commonly seen on the heaths. The more widespread common species flowers in the spring and then by late summer, when the terrain turns purple

A male adder is resplendent in its colours after shedding its skin.

with flowering heather, another flush of yellow bloom from the more dainty western gorse emerges, adding more vibrancy to the scene.

One creature that welcomes the coming of spring to the heaths is the adder. To find one, pick a warm day and visit mid morning to early afternoon in March and April and search carefully in the leaf litter or open short grass at the base of gorse and bramble patches or amidst clearings in the heather. This is the preferred time and place to look for the males as they will have just emerged from their mid winter retreat in underground hibernacula and now need all the warmth from the sun to revitalise their skin and attain peak breeding condition. Early in the season the males can be quite lethargic, lying coiled up often close to regularly used footpaths where they will allow a very close approach, providing the observer treads slowly and carefully. Disturb them and all you may see is one disappearing for cover or into an old rabbit burrow (a favoured place for hibernating adders) with a surprisingly fast and smooth escape, its coils and body contortions moving seamlessly over whatever obstacle is in its path. In the mid twentieth century adders were regularly sought out at Syderstone and the nearby Coxford Heath (two heathland sites in the west of the region) by boys who would gain extra pocket money by 'collecting' adders as they emerged from hibernation, their skins sought after by the shoe trade. Thankfully this pursuit is long in the past and adders are now totally protected by law.

The male adder times his return to the outside world a few weeks before the first female is seen and he uses this time to prepare himself for the imminent breeding season. When newly emerged he will be a dull brown creature with darker zigzag markings on his back, mixed in with a greyer tone along his sides, blending perfectly with the dead leaves and fronds of bracken of late winter. Before he reaches the peak of his condition he has to shed his skin, after which he transforms into a startlingly bright and strikingly marked snake. The shiny pale greenish-white body with bold black 'v's down his back and peppered along his flanks are all set off by vivid golden orange eyes. Now his colours blend more with the newly sprouting grasses.

Revitalised and resplendent, the male adder then becomes far more active, looking more vigilant and moving with great purpose as he attempts to find a mate. Female adders are larger and have a different mix of oranges and browns and, as they do not breed every year, only those which are ready to mate, emerge early. There are usually more males than females and consequently there is serious competition in the quest to win a mate. This is when male adders begin to 'dance', which is another of the English countryside's greatest spectacles. Upon meeting, the two male adders will size each other up; they dart one way and then the other with flicking tongues and eyes wide open and alert before they make contact. Then they glide through the undergrowth with bodies pressed together trying to push the other away. Then, suddenly, one will rear up, only for its movements instantly to be copied by its opponent. A great deal of pushing and writhing then gets underway, usually in an upright position although sometimes they move along without touching. Usually they will end up almost locked together with their heads held erect and both looking in the same forward direction. Surprisingly, biting seldom occurs and the victor is the one that raises itself highest and manages to push its opponent's head down the hardest.

When a male has attained his dominance and found a female, a fast moving courtship chase will follow. The male effortlessly follows the female's every move until she finally accepts him and the pair entwine and mate. From then on, adders become much more elusive, living a solitary existence and feeding on a variety of prey such as small mammals, lizards and even nestling birds. By late summer young adders can be encountered, although good breeding years often result in high mortality particularly if a minor road bisects a major piece of heathland. During the last warm days of autumn there may be the sight of an adder basking in the sun again, but for most, it will be the end of a brief busy year as hibernation once more beckons.

The female adder is larger and browner in colour than a male.

There are a number of specialised insects that find the dry sandy conditions of the heaths and the unique vegetation to their liking. One of the most striking butterflies is the green hairstreak, unmistakable as it is the only British species that is predominantly green. It is the undersides of the wings that are green and as the butterfly invariably rests with its wings closed there should be no mistaking one when seen. This small insect is on the wing in late April and never far away from either gorse or broom, where it lays its eggs.

Another butterfly that can be seen at Kelling Heath is the silver-studded blue. While green hairstreaks can be also be found at other wooded localities in the county, the silver-studded blue is a true heathland specialist tied to the heather, bracken and gorse on which it lays its eggs. This beautiful butterfly is more abundant in southern England, but even here its numbers have been in serious decline as a result of habitat destruction. In Norfolk, with few pristine heaths left, the story has been the same and many naturalists feared that if action was not taken local extinction might not be far away. Successful translocation and colony formation occurred on some sites close to Norwich and with this in mind it was decided that Kelling Heath would be another likely spot for a population - despite the insect having disappeared from there in the 1970s. A greater management initiative was started in the 1990s, creating more open heather habitat and in 2001 the first re-introductions were made. These proved so successful that it is once more possible to witness extraordinary numbers of these busy little blue butterflies drifting over the heather in July.

The green hairstreak is a beautiful, yet tiny butterfly and easily seen in the spring.

Small skipper feeding on bell heather

Below: The silver-studded blue butterfly has been successfully re-introduced to Kelling.

Green tiger beetles are easily seen on the open sandy paths of the area's heaths.

Another insect that can be encountered quite easily on the heaths is the green tiger beetle. Like the green hairstreak it too is a lovely iridescent green, but it is a voracious predator, often seen scuttling across open sandy areas or with a buzzing flight over the heaths. It has large eyes relative to its size and fierce looking jaws which it regularly utilises when it comes upon any suitable insect prey. Look out for bloody-nosed beetles; rotund, and flightless they have a peculiar habit of secreting blood from their mouths if alarmed. Minotaur beetles also love the open terrain and are equally intriguing as they frequently bury rabbit droppings on which their larvae then feed.

Many naturalists that visit North Norfolk come to see the specialist heathland birds. Nightingales have long been a traditional species for birdwatchers to seek out during their brief but captivating springtime song period in April and May when the blackthorn scrub on the edge of the heaths offers a favourite site for these secretive songsters. Like the nightingale, two other equally fine song birds also migrate from Africa, the blackcap and garden warbler, and they too can be seen around the more scrubby woodland margins of heathland. Other more localised residents such as redpolls, woodcock and long-eared owls can be seen with luck or patience, although the first is becoming decidedly rare as a breeding species these days. All of these species are present in other wooded localities but there is, however, one species that constantly attracts a procession of admirers throughout its summer stay and is tied almost solely to heathland here in North Norfolk. For the nightjar, a mysterious migrant with nocturnal habits, Salthouse and Kelling heaths provide its only regular haunts.

Nightjars are almost like the bats of the bird world as they emerge at dusk to hunt for insects over the heaths with a complete mastery of aerial manoeuvres. For most people, however, the sight of a hunting nightjar will perhaps be a long time coming. It needs time and patience to gain a good view, only possible in that brief spell of twilight before darkness envelopes the open heath. To hear one, however, is far easier as they can often be heard uttering their very unusual purring, rhythmic 'chur' all through the night. This unmistakable song is often uttered from the ground but sometimes from the branches of an exposed tree that so often punctuates the open heathland landscape. Old local names such as 'scissor- and razor- grinder' were a testament to the almost constant mechanical like noise that is very much the sound of a summer's night on a heath.

Whilst many may only gain a fleeting view of a dark shape twisting and turning with scythe like wings, their silhouette sometimes enlivened by the white wing and tail patches of the male, to gain a view in daytime is even more fortunate. Then nightjars remain hidden to all but the most skilled, patient or lucky observers. They choose to nest in an open spot with stones, twigs and bracken fronds where their cryptic grey and brown plumage makes as excellent a form of camouflage displayed by any bird. In reality it is best not to search for them in the day as they can soon be disturbed and eggs can be trampled by unwary feet. Instead take time to enjoy them at their best, 'churring' on a moonlit night and hawking for insects. Then they truly are masters of the night sky.

With all the management work that our heaths have received since the 1990s, creating tree-less tracts with a dominant ground cover of heather, it is pleasing to see that certain characteristic species have either returned or increased in numbers. Woodlarks, the heathland counterpart of skylarks, were one of the first specialist species to reappear on the north coast heaths, albeit in very small numbers. For much of the latter half of the twentieth century, woodlarks were confined in Norfolk to Breckland and it was not until the 1990s that the first north coast breeding birds reclaimed their old haunts. As well as loving pure heathland, woodlarks are also quick to move in to woodland that has been cleared of conifers and even occasionally on coastal dunes, such as at Holkham where a pair nested on two occasions in the past.

On the ground their appearance may only seem subtly different from their common relative but in flight they look much shorter tailed. This gives them a somewhat bat-like look, particularly when they are sailing around at a great height singing. The woodlark's song is a sweet sounding mixture of trills and warbling that ends with a distinctive descending flurry of flute-like notes and to many it is the sound of a hot summer's day on a heath. On still moonlit nights some woodlarks actually continue to sing until the early hours of the morning, almost outdoing the nightingales that may also be uttering their own spring serenades.

A typical view of a 'churring' nightjar on an exposed perch at dusk.

Another species to return to Norfolk in recent times is the Dartford warbler. It is one of Britain's few resident warblers, and was once restricted to southern England. This delightful long tailed grey and plum coloured bird has been spreading into East Anglia since the 1990s, helped it is thought by rising temperatures and milder winters. It was very fitting that this heather loving species should re-establish itself in Norfolk at Kelling Heath during 2007. Although the population is at present very small, the birds presence is encouraging for numbers to increase in the future. Apart from when in song, the Dartford warbler can be very elusive and a somewhat easier species to see is the stonechat. One advantage is that Dartford warblers often associate with stonechats, taking small insect prey items that the larger birds disturb.

Stonechats were once said to be widespread over Norfolk in the wild spots of open ground where gorse was abundant. The habitat loss and colder winters of earlier times, however, caused their disappearance from the county as a breeding species by the middle of the twentieth century. Recently, however, the stonechats fortunes have taken a turn for the better. They have re-established themselves in North Norfolk, thanks not only to habitat improvement but also probably to the milder winters. Up until the 1990s, these birds were usually associated with the winter months, when a handful of migrant birds would appear on coastal sand dunes and in reed beds. A notable passage would also occur in late February – March: some no doubt British birds heading back to their upland breeding grounds, others going to the coasts of the near continent. Either way their numbers were increasing and it was not too long before the first pairs found new places to nest. Following sporadic nesting attempts throughout the 1970s and 1980s, Stonechats finally became residents again by the late 1990s, breeding not only on the heaths but also in coastal dune scrub.

A male stonechat singing from the top of a gorse bush.

A typical piece of modern North Norfolk farmland near East Barsham.

Chapter Nine

An ever changing farmland

Much of Norfolk is dominated by agriculture; indeed up to 80% of its land is farmed. It is also often labelled as 'flat' as its highest point only reaches 100 metres above sea level inland from Sheringham. Unfortunately such conditions can delude some visitors into thinking that a large part of Norfolk, away from the immediate coastline is a somewhat uninteresting place. This of course is far from the case. North Norfolk is certainly not flat like the fens; it has a gently undulating landscape and for those with time and patience there is much to be gained inland by seeking out the subtleties of a more overlooked part of the local countryside. Once again North Norfolk is very fortunate, for within view of the coast there are serene river valleys, mature hedgerows, mixed woodland and parks of open grassland, all tucked neatly into a patchwork of farmland. Equally as encouraging is that in this intensively managed agricultural heartland, some typical farmland birds and animals still remain at much higher densities than in other parts of the county.

Norfolk's long agricultural history dates back much further than the meticulously worked arable fields of today. Our primitive ancestors were responsible for clearing the forests of lowland Britain and by the time of the Romans, the east coast was valued not only for cereal production but also for exporting grain from the coastal ports. By the Middle Ages sheep had become immensely important, with Norfolk becoming very prosperous thanks to wool production. Even the poor heathland soil that made up much of the coast's hinterland proved to be valuable such was its suitability for grazing sheep. The wealth generated is reflected to this day by the grand churches in relatively small villages dotted along the coast. Blakeney, Brancaster, Cley, Salthouse and Wiveton were all important ports for the thriving wool trade while the stately hall at East Barsham was built from the profits of sheep farming. Other land such as the chalky boulder clays in the west proved more suitable for cereal farming and crops such as barley (of which much was exported), oats, wheat and rye were all grown and helped its landowners to become prosperous.

This period of wealth advanced further still thanks to the innovations and progress made by wealthy landowners such as Viscount Charles Townsend of Raynham (near Fakenham) and Viscount Thomas Coke (later the Earl of Leicester) of Holkham. Townshend is credited with the introduction in the 1730s of the 'Norfolk Four Course' rotation of crops. Variations of this rotation were to remain the basis of Norfolk farming for the next 200 years. Typically, a crop of wheat was followed by one of turnips folded with sheep whose dung fertilized the field; next came barley, and then, to complete the rotation, a crop of clover - the nitrogen fixing properties of which enriched the soil ready for another crop of wheat.

When Thomas Coke inherited his Holkham estate in 1776, the soil was so poor that it was said that 'two rabbits could be seen fighting for one blade of grass'. By adopting new techniques and practices such as the four course rotation, and by liberally spreading on his fields the chalky clay ('marl') that lay beneath the generally light and acidic top-soils, he greatly increased the productivity of his land. Disused marl pits, often containing small clumps of trees, are still to be seen in many North Norfolk fields. Coke's improvements enabled him greatly to increase not only the yields of his crops but also the stocking rates of his sheep and cattle, and his insistence that his tenants should follow his example meant that in forty years the rent-roll of the estate increased from £2,200 to £20,000.

The widespread adoption of the new agricultural practices, the development of improved machinery (such as the iron plough first produced in 1770), the consolidation of agricultural holdings (which led to the demise of the ancient strip fields) and the enclosure of common land during the Napoleonic Wars led to Norfolk becoming a county dominated by arable agriculture. By the end of the eighteenth century two thirds of its land was in arable cropping and three quarters of this was in large fields enclosed by hedges. Cereal yields were greatly increased and more grain was exported from Norfolk than from the rest of England put together.

The increase in the profitability of agriculture further increased the landowners' prosperity enabling them to spend more on their large estates, laying out formal gardens and landscaping of their parks. Holkham is a prime example of this and has been much written about. Within its 3000 acres there are woods, arable fields, a lake, a deer park, an imposing hall, an obelisk, a temple, follies and farm buildings.

Holkham was not alone and other similar estates such as Raynham, Houghton, Bayfield and Sandringham to name but a few are all within a relatively short distance of the North Norfolk coast. Neither was the idea of a deer park unique as its concept dates back to Norman times when fallow deer were stocked in large enclosures thus allowing protection and a regular hunting quarry for the landowner. Today in Norfolk only Holkham, Houghton, Melton Constable and Gunton remain from a list of almost one hundred deer parks in the county. Holkham's well watched deer population actually dates back to the mid 1700s when a nine mile wall effectively enclosed the park and fallow deer were stocked from an older established park at North Elmham. To this day a herd of several hundred still occupy the lightly wooded grassland where for the most part they live totally wild, the only concession being a bit of extra food if hard winter weather prevails. Fallow deer are actually quite scarce away from the parks and the small pockets of groups that do exist, are all as a result of escapes.

Fallow deer have been in Britain since Norman times although the Holkham herd has only been in residence since the 1700s.

Red deer these days can be seen in small, very mobile herds around the woods and fields inland, some even venturing onto coastal marshes and beaches where their large hoof prints quickly betray their presence. Despite their imposing size they can remain surprisingly elusive, only venturing into open ground at dusk and dawn. These too are undoubtedly strays from parks, as Melton Constable, Houghton and Gunton all traditionally kept small numbers of these impressive animals. It is only since the new millennium, however, that Holkham has begun to keep red deer.

Many of the large, landscaped parks with their clumps and belts of trees, walled gardens and follies also had a lake which became home to an ornamental wildfowl collection. One species that was frequently introduced and has since staked its claim as a naturalised Norfolk resident, personifying the parkland scenery that has become its well suited home, is the Egyptian goose.

Since its initial introduction into Britain from the lakes of sub-Saharan Africa towards the end of the seventeenth century it has adapted well to the changed environment and it has become as much a part of the countryside as have other such introductions, be they pheasants, gadwall, little owls, red-legged partridges, rabbits or fallow deer. In fact, whilst many view it as an obtrusive alien, the Egyptian goose has actually been naturalised here longer than either the little owl or gadwall; two species many people fail to realise were not always native to our land.

North Norfolk has since become the stronghold of the British population of the Egyptian goose and it is Holkham Park that holds the largest concentration. Up to 15 pairs annually rear their young in the open deciduous woodland surrounding the lake. Here they seek out large cavities in the trunks of mature beech, chestnut and oak trees in which to nest. If the sight of such a seemingly cumbersome bird, clambering about on the branches of a mature tree is not

Holkham Lake is one of the best sites in Britain for breeding and moulting Egyptian geese.

enough, the fact that the species invariably nests very early in the year makes them even more remarkable. Sometimes the first fledglings appear in January or February, although March and April are the most likely times for the tiny pied balls of fluff to appear from their lofty nest sites, before they are shepherded to the nearest water.

Broods may number as many as 15 goslings and such large numbers seem essential, as chick mortality is usually high. By mid June to August, most of the region's Egyptian geese head for Holkham Lake, where they traditionally congregate to moult. Occasionally close on 300 birds have been counted, the lake obviously offering safety for the short period when feathers are shed and the geese become flightless.

With country estates fast becoming affluent and fashionable the popularity of shooting pheasants began to gather pace throughout the 1800s and it was the rich gentry who paid handsomely to participate in the shoots. Big bags meant high dividends and fame for the estate that could produce the most. At Holkham one of the old game books logged over 104,000 pheasants shot over 30 winters beginning in 1900. From humble beginnings as an additional food source to the Romans who first brought them to this country from the woodlands of Asia, pheasants have pretty much shaped and dictated the fortunes of many of our native birds. A greater surplus of birds was required for the winter shooting season than would ever be attained in a fully natural environment and this meant that many typical natural predators of the countryside were obsessively controlled. Stoats, hedgehogs, foxes, badgers, birds of prey and members of the crow family were all deemed as unwanted vermin that had to be exterminated from the countryside.

While it is true that predators can have an impact on ground nesting birds, the fact that nearly all of the Norfolk countryside began to revolve around shooting made it very difficult for predatory species to survive. A black period in Norfolk's conservation story began which never

The fox remains as it always has, one of the countryside's most persistant predators.

really ended until comparatively modern times. Any bird with a hooked beak was hated, and it seemed second nature that any owl or raptor should be shot, trapped or poisoned.

In Victorian times and even through much of the twentieth century, the only certain way to see a bird such as a buzzard was to find it swinging from a pole trap or hanging on a gamekeeper's trophy line. Buzzards were, until recent times, always viewed as being very scarce visitors to North Norfolk, which made the shooting of four from an unprecedented ten wintering in Holkham Park in 1931 even more inexcusable. It also illustrates perfectly how the general attitude was so fixed in these now antiquated values. With buzzards feeding on carrion, rabbits, rodents and even earth worms the damage they would have caused to the local game population would have been negligible. Thankfully attitudes are better these days and many landowners display a much more enlightened view on birds of prey. Buzzards now seem to be a permanent fixture in the local countryside since they first nested near Holkham Park in 1993. Since then numbers have risen in North Norfolk to about 30 pairs, a true testament to the hard work conservationists undertook to ensure the legal protection of owls and raptors and ultimately the space they are now given by game keepers and landowners.

It is not only buzzards that have spread. Since the mid 1980s, marsh harriers arrived from the coast and began nesting in autumn sown cereals and fields of rape. Sparrowhawks have risen in numbers following almost complete annihilation during the days of rampant persecution and the widespread use of the chemical DDT in the 1970s which led to eggs being laid with thin shells. These days they nest in most wooded areas. The hobby, a small dashing falcon that arrives for the summer to prey upon dragonflies and birds such as swifts and swallows, was once restricted to the southern English heaths but since the 1990s it too is a regular sight over the farmland of North Norfolk. Even badgers which, locally, were once pretty much confined to the Wensum valley between Fakenham and Norwich, now inhabit many an old marl pit or

This sparrowhawk caught this lapwing with ease, although on this occasion its prey had a lucky escape.

woodland edge in North Norfolk. Predators and their prey species can live together providing there is plenty of habitat to support all of them.

For all the negatives the countryside gained in the wanton persecution of predators, it is also true to say that many of the woods and copses of North Norfolk would have long gone if it were not for the incentive provided by game rearing and shooting. By doing so, many farmers and landowners have maintained significant populations of other woodland birds, mammals and wild flowers. Today many shoots have progressed to carrying out worthwhile woodland management in the hope that more wildlife can be encouraged and it is certain that many declining species of song birds do benefit from the additional feeding stations that are provided for pheasants.

While pheasants were an introduced quarry, other resident species were shot over the winter sporting period. The grey partridge is North Norfolk's only true native game bird and it was also once the most widespread and common of Britain's game birds. Its numbers were probably at their peak in the 1700s and 1800s when agricultural practises began to become organised and more efficient. The introduction of crop rotations saw peas and beans grown regularly for the first time alongside fields of lay grass and cereals, all of which added to the partridge's food supply. Also the planting of many hedges as field borders created plenty of sites where the females could lay their large clutch of eggs. The fact that everywhere was also well keepered meant that one of the partridge's most persistent foes, the fox, was low in numbers. Today's problems such as disturbance from people with unlimited leisure time, dogs to walk and free access to the countryside was then virtually unheard of.

Unfortunately the intensification of farming methods has paved the way for a dramatic decline in numbers; a problem that has become progressively worse since the Second World War. Chemical pesticides and herbicides were introduced to produce greater yields and

A covey of grey partridges cower into the snow, ever alert for predators.

healthier crops, and hedgerows were uprooted to make the way for bigger farm machinery. The consequence is that the grey partridge has lost much of its nesting habitat and the weeds that provided an abundance of insect life have disappeared from the intensively sprayed crops. In recent years the lack of insect prey has been combined with cold wet spells in June and for many of the chicks their chances of survival became slight. Such factors have led the population to plummet by 82% between 1970 and 1998, a devastating drop for a bird that was once shot in vast numbers. The days when 186 were shot by a single gun over an eight hour period on October 7th 1797 within a square mile at Warham and a record 1671 from the whole of the Warham parish on a single day in 1905 are long in the past. North Norfolk is fortunate that it still has a good population of partridges from which it can build upon. Numbers are said to be the best in Britain, with an estate like Holkham still having an estimated population of 600 pairs in 2008. Some estates now either prevent grey partridge shooting or have strict bag limits, measures that are definitely a positive way forward if the species is to survive.

The grey partridge is a bird that always seems to look at its best in the late winter and spring. By then the family coveys from the previous year's breeding will be splitting up, leaving pairs to form and the males to cry out their rasping 'song'. Like cock pheasants, the males fight furiously to guard or acquire a mate. They move at an amazing pace, wheeling into the air as they try to grab each other; the victor determinedly chasing after his opponent. To see a male bird standing proudly alongside his crouching mate is one of the finest sights in our arable landscape and it is up to the farmers, landowners and conservationists to make a grand effort and ensure that the grey partridge does not disappear.

In contrast to the well studied grey partridge, the woodcock is an altogether more mysterious bird, with a secretive life spent mostly hidden in the understorey of woodland. A crepuscular lifestyle and a highly camouflaged russet brown plumage makes it for many observers about as co-operative as a bittern in a reed bed. Small numbers breed in our

This woodcock is seen adopting a rarely observed full threat posture. In the autumn newly arrived migrants can be uncharacteristically tame.

woodlands, although finding a nest in leaf litter surrounded by brambles or dog's mercury is an achievement very few experience. Instead, a good indication of a breeding population is the dawn and dusk display flights of the male. His regular flight over woods (known as roding) whilst uttering a peculiar squeaking and grunting sound is his way of finding a mate and alerting other males of his presence. It is a sure sign that spring has arrived and often the only indication that a breeding woodcock is present. As male woodcock are polygamous and often undertake long and varied display flight routes, judging the precise size of a breeding population is often impossible.

Migrant woodcock arrive from the continent every autumn during northerly and easterly winds and further numbers occur during mid-winter cold snaps. It is then when they are shot sometimes in large numbers during pheasant shoots in our woodland and it is usually only then when an indication of the numbers present can be gleaned. Woodcock shooting has always played a big part of the local estates, perhaps more so in the past than today. Chantry Hills, a wood on the Holkham estate, was actually named after the gentleman (a Lord Chantry) who shot a brace of woodcock with a blast from each barrel. The feat was even immortalised in a small book of poetry written by some of his colleagues describing the event.

Counts of 3000 shot at Holkham between 1900 and 1930, with 334 shot in the autumn of 1925 alone, gives an indication of the numbers present in the past and also the amount that were slaughtered. Numbers have undoubtedly been less in recent years due perhaps to milder winters although 1997 was an exception when at least 1000 were present at Holkham in January, of which 140 were shot over three days. At least some local estates refuse to shoot them and such actions should be applauded and more widely applied. For such a beautiful, intricately marked wading bird, whose true status remains unknown the ultimate answer should really be total, legal protection.

Barn owls regularly hunt the grass verges alongside the roads and lanes of North Norfolk.

There is one bird of prey that unlike many of its relatives faced very little persecution in its rural surroundings. It is the one species that everyone seems to love. Most farmers and landowners who have it nest on their land or in their buildings are proud and protective of it. Birdwatchers never tire of watching it, particularly visitors from other parts of the country where it is seldom seen, and even gamekeepers, many whom for the most part still despise any bird with a hooked beak, appreciate it. It is a species long associated with the folklore of rural England and so loved due to its ghost like qualities that even those who know little of its habits or are even remotely interested in wildlife recognise it as being something quite special. That bird is the barn owl and here in North Norfolk we are exceptionally lucky as it is one of the most characteristic specialities of the area's farmland.

The barn owl is the easiest of its family to be seen in North Norfolk and although it is a nocturnal hunter, it is particularly active around sunrise and sunset and also frequently hunts during the day. It can commonly be seen during long light summer evenings when it is facing the extra burden of feeding its fledglings, and also in the daytime during the winter when a combination of low prey density and bad weather will dictate a change in habits. Barn owls cannot cope so well in heavy rain or in saturated undergrowth as they have less oil in their plumage than many birds, while the movement of their prey may also be restricted then. In the snow or after penetrating frosts and during windy nights an even more daunting spell of hunting may be faced. Life can really be tough for barn owls in such conditions and then they may be forced to spend most of the subsequent day searching for prey.

North Norfolk's countryside really does seem ideal for barn owls. Numerous lanes and roads dissect a rural landscape of woods, copses, meadows, marshes and arable land. The roadside verges are often wide with a lush growth of grass, ideal habitat for short-tailed field voles, one of the owl's principal food items. In contrast, the large and intensively farmed blocks of North

Norfolk's arable land provide very little to attract rodents, which makes the grassy corridors of its hedgerows and roadside verges an extremely important habitat for barn owls to feed in.

Apart from grassland to hunt, barn owls also require plenty of nesting and roosting sites. With the North Norfolk countryside full of grand old barns and farm complexes, some dating back to the 1700s there has never been any shortage of such requirements. Hedgerows liberally dotted with mature oak and ash trees (and in earlier times, elms) are just as important to the barn owl. This was highlighted in 1990 when the Hawk and Owl Trust carried out a survey of nesting barn owls in North Norfolk and from 92 confirmed breeding sites, 39 were in old farm buildings and the other 53 were all in tree cavities.

Sadly in many parts of the country a decline in barn owl numbers has occurred, with the UK population dropping by 69% between the 1930s and the 1980s, and there seem just as many threats present today as in the past. One of the greatest causes of concern is the number of owls that perish on the roads. With such a widespread swathe of prey-rich habitat as the roadside verges it is hardly surprising that many meet their demise after drifting into fast moving traffic. While this modern threat looks certain never to go away, fluctuations in rodent populations can also greatly affect barn owl survival rates. In a poor year the mortality of young owls rises significantly and it is not too unusual to find the terribly thin corpse of an owl that has starved to death. On the other hand barn owls can thrive if there is plenty of food and will continue breeding all year round if such conditions prevail.

Barn owls frequently hunt during the day particularly after wet and windy nights.

Farmyards such as this are becoming a rarity in Norfolk in recent years as many are converted to living accommodation and become unsuitable for nesting barn owls.

Since the 1800s when the countryside was gripped by agricultural change, many meadows have been ploughed, marshes drained and conifer woods planted, all depriving the barn owl of precious hunting areas. In the 1960s and 1970s cases of secondary poisoning started to arise from the use of chemical poisons aimed at rats and mice. Nest and roost sites have been lost with the felling of mature trees and although the practise of uprooting miles of hedgerows had its days in the 1970s, these days many diseased or rotten trees are singled out as roadside hazards, once more depriving the owl of a home.

The farmyards and barns of North Norfolk have also undergone great changes since the late 1980s. Many were unable to provide access for large modern machinery, some were deemed unhygienic and too damp for grain storage and livestock became uneconomically viable to rear. As a result many stood empty in disrepair and were a sad sign of changing times in farming. The demise of farms with livestock along with the ultra careful clean and tidy environment of modern health and safety conscious farmers means that there is very little spilt grain and unwanted rodents are often eradicated by more clinical means. Many barns have been restored and converted into living accommodation and although such work is supposed to take into consideration the needs of owls, more often than not it is the barn owl that loses out. The provision of nest boxes has been quite successful in many cases, but with the immediate surroundings no longer being suitable for feeding, the farms and barns as many knew them have all but disappeared. Indeed some parts of Norfolk are not the ideal haven for the barn owl that they once were.

Another owl that is present in North Norfolk is the little owl. Little owls also love to nest in old trees and there are many hedgerows away from the coast that offer them nesting and roosting opportunities. Despite this they can often be very elusive, being most active at dawn and dusk when many moths are on the wing - the owl's favoured food along with earthworms and beetles. Late summer remains the best time for regular observations as this is when the noisy youngsters are beginning to leave their nests. Then they are easy to see, often sitting out in the open in full sun, always ready to clumsily greet a returning parent carrying a beak full of food. Apart from hedgerows, little owls make use of old buildings and the disused airbases of North Norfolk always offer plenty of suitable nest sites.

A little owl perched on top of an old barn roof, close to its nest site.

An alert hare sitting in a stubble field.

The hare is one creature that really took advantage of the large arable fields of North Norfolk and has become an integral part of our rural landscape. Since the Second World War, however, the country has lost roughly 75% of its hares. Changes in agricultural practices such as the use of chemical sprays, larger farm machinery, hedgerow removal, setting light to stubble fields, overshooting by hunters, a rise in fox numbers and wet weather in the spring have all added to their problems.

In some parts of south west England hares have all but disappeared but here in North Norfolk they still thrive, particularly on the light sandy loams of our arable fields. Numbers remain sufficiently high for them still to be a common sight and for those who regularly watch them they are a spectacular component of the local countryside. Hares are not an easy subject to study due to their secretive manners. They are animals that are very active at night, feeding both themselves and their offspring. A female may have three or more litters per year with usually three offspring per litter, although sometimes five or six and these are usually suckled from dusk onwards. Young hares or leverets are different from young rabbits in that they are born above the ground instead of in burrows, have all their fur (instead of being naked) and have their lovely blue-grey eyes wide open from birth.

Most youngsters try to remain hidden from any potential predators by sitting tight, usually (but not always) scattered apart in low depressions and often concealed by a tussock of grass or any other suitable vegetation. By splitting up her litter and only returning to them as darkness falls, the mother hopefully ensures a greater chance of survival. This of course is difficult with there being so many predators about both on the ground and from the air above. Countless numbers undoubtedly perish, not only from predation but also from the large agricultural machines that constantly crawl across the land. It has been said that up to 90% of young hares die within a year of being born. Even old hares would rather sit tight at frighteningly close distances to working tractors, thinking they are safe, rather than run off and give away their presence.

Two very young leverets hidden in their 'form', oblivious to an oncoming tractor.

Male hares are renowned for their promiscuity and by late winter will be looking to mate with any number of females. This is a time of great activity. It is not unusual to see gangs, sometimes up to a dozen, chasing and frolicking on open cereal fields, vying for the female's attention. When she does appear, pandemonium sets in as frenzied pursuits begin. This is when 'boxing' is most likely to be witnessed although this is a part of the hare's life that is not just restricted to March (as many people seem to believe) and can be seen at nearly anytime of the year; albeit with a peak in late winter-early spring. Another misconception is that boxing hares are always two aggressive males fighting to win the females attention. In reality it is usually the female who rears up on her hind legs to see off a male whom she does not like the look of. Males will of course fight and this can usually be seen when several are pursuing one female. When boxing, hares leap up into the air; they frantically strike and scratch with their front paws sending fur flying before chasing off to have another bout elsewhere in the field. Watching boxing hares can provide tense, dramatic moments and is one countryside spectacle that should not be missed.

Game books on some of the large estates give an idea of the numbers that can be present, particularly when it has been estimated that over 50% of the area's hares can survive an organised cull. Numbers were probably at their peak in the late 1800s, when at Holkham for example, over 1200 were shot on one day in December 1877 by 11 shooters. This was a phenomenal number especially considering that over 1000 had already been shot over the previous five days. Other counts from that period illustrate that to shoot over 1000 during a winter monthly period was not unusual. These days many North Norfolk estates will shoot up to 300 in a day if they are lucky and probably never more than 1000 in a season. There are some estates and farms that do not shoot hares, arguing that they are a species in need of protection and space to find their own population levels. Here they have become far less wary and sometimes larger than average numbers build up. One such area close to South Creake is a fantastic place for observing hares and it is often possible to count up to 90 animals spread over two adjacent fields on a summer's evening.

Boxing hares produce one of the greatest spectacles of a spring day on North Norfolk's farmland.

Crop spraying at Beacon Hill near Burnham Market.

So with an abundance of hares, barn owls and growing numbers of raptors soaring over the fields all would appear to be well. Yet this is not quite the case. Of all the habitats of North Norfolk it is farmland that has undergone the most change. Farming thrived in the late 1700s and early 1800s thanks not only to the innovative methods employed to improve yields but also a food shortage in Britain due to the Napoleonic Wars blocking foreign imports. This had all but changed by the late 1800s when the area was gripped by agricultural depression due to foreign competition and falling grain prices. Many farms fell into a state of disrepair whilst others diversified into livestock farming once more, the result being the re-establishment of much semi permanent meadowland. With the advent of the First World War arable farming once more began to dominate the land, with sugar beet (first grown here in 1912) becoming an important crop. This once more triggered a decline in sheep farming.

More modern times have seen a greater usage of sprays and fertilizers, thus rendering the old system of crop rotation all but redundant. In addition bigger machinery has meant even bigger fields and in the 1970s there was a universal trend for hedgerow removal to allow ease of access for such machines (half of Norfolk's hedges disappeared between the 1940s and the 1970s). The switch to autumn sown crops and the subsequent lack of stubble fields over winter, the disappearance of imposing straw and hay stacks, and the increasing acreage of oil seed rape and other biofuel crops have all contributed to making the modern rural landscape a completely different one to that of only 50 years ago.

With such changes it is perhaps little wonder that the wildlife of rural Norfolk has undergone great change. It is very sad that once common farmland birds are disappearing, some at an alarming rate. One species that has almost disappeared is the tree sparrow. This rural relative of the house sparrow with its smart chestnut crown and black cheek spot was once a common bird found widely throughout North Norfolk. Every farmyard and isolated barn had its own

Above: A newly prepared carrot field near North Creake, complete with a prospecting lapwing.

Below: Tree sparrows were once abundant in North Norfolk. Sadly numbers are now perilously low.

flock and during the winter these frequently joined up to form larger gatherings on stubble fields and around winter stock enclosures. Up to the 1980s, noisy flocks of up to 100 strong were a common sight around the livestock and farm buildings in Holkham Park, yet none have nested there since 1993. Similar numbers were present everywhere and the largest single flock on record is the 1500 that were at Cley in the winter of 1958. Since the late 1980s this decline has meant that there may only be two or three flocks in the whole of the area and if their numbers reach double figures they are worthy of note. What is even more worrying is that the disappearance of the tree sparrow is not restricted to Norfolk; between 1970 and 1998 the entire British population had declined by 95%. Some hope has been gained at farms such as Courtyard Farm at Ringstead where nest boxes have been provided and allowed a population of 16-17 pairs (in the years 2005 – 2008) to hang on. As the farm also uses organic practices, it perhaps points to a way forward for other farms and estates to follow.

While the tree sparrow's decline was deemed to be a sorry state of affairs and a sad reflection of many of the countryside's problems, when its common counterpart the house sparrow started to go the same way, conservationists really started to worry. In the 1970s it would have been almost impossible to imagine a farmyard without tree sparrows and absolutely unthinkable to find one without its own colony of house sparrows. After all, this was a species whose resilience and adaptability has enabled it to colonize much of the modern world. Numbers were often so great locally that their constant chattering was often considered to be an undesirable din. This was particularly so when large flocks at the end of the breeding season descended onto stubble fields and around straw stacks after the summer harvest. Many were targeted as pests and shot as the flocks left their roosts or landed to feed on vegetable gardens or village allotments. Even as recently as the late 1970s, local game dealers selling to the French market, paid as little as three pence for each house sparrow they received in contrast to

This flock of house sparrows on autumn stubble near Great Walsingham in 1996 was a sight that was once commonplace. Today it is virtually impossible to find.

five pence per starling, 25 pence per wood pigeon and 40 pence per rabbit. By the late 1990s, however, it became clear that numbers were disappearing, again at a fast rate. Town and village sparrows are also declining but not to the extent of the farmland ones and there are now very few farms or barns that have remained attractive to sparrows. To many people it seems unbelievable that a bird once so abundant should be declining at such a rate.

Other species are also no longer so abundant. Yellowhammers were once one of the most numerous farmland songbirds. In the breeding season every green lane and hedgerow boasted significant numbers of these cheery songsters and in the winter months almost every farmyard or stubble field would host a flock. Despite a farm such as Courtyard at Ringstead (covering close on 800 acres) still managing to attract 42 pairs in 2008, overall, Yellowhammers are in a state of continuing decline.

In the 1950s, starlings blackened the skies when over three million descended into communal winter roosts around Egmere although those days are long gone. Even the breeding numbers are a fraction of those in the past. Neither is this decline restricted to our resident birds for the turtle dove, which migrates here every spring from African wintering grounds to nest in thick mature thorn hedges, is also fast disappearing. With their soft purring songs and delightful plumage these little doves are amongst the most beautiful of their family, yet unfortunately immense numbers are being slaughtered as they migrate through southern Europe, so much so that their population has dropped by up to 80%.

Since the late 1980s a number of schemes have been trialled in the hope of creating a lifeline for our resident farmland birds. The provision of six metre wide unsprayed margins and game cover strips, for example, provides additional cover not only for game birds in the winter but for songbirds too. Many of the introduced crops such as maize, *quinoa*, sunflowers and *phacelia* set along field headlands have the additional advantage of producing good quantities of seeds

Yellowhammers feeding in a Hindringham farmyard.

Two courting turtle doves.
Numbers are dwindling due to shooting on their continental migration routes.

that flocks of buntings, finches and sparrows can feast on. Thankfully many estates have also begun replanting hedges. Uncultivated field margins and set-aside projects, in which fields have been left fallow for a season or sometimes longer have proved beneficial, allowing many wild flowers (often agricultural 'weeds' such as poppies and corn marigolds) to re-establish themselves. This creates habitat for insects and in turn food for birds. Continual politically dictated changes in farming policies, however, have meant that nothing so far has been left long enough for really positive results to emerge and reverse the downward fortunes of our farmland birds. Even birds such as the wintering pinkfeet geese that flock here in tens of thousands could become a thing of the past if we are not careful. Their future seems linked too close for comfort to the decisions of politicians and farming policies. Lowering sugar beet prices, changing quotas and the importing of sugar cane could all have a significant impact on the geese that rely on the wastage of the harvest for their survival. Despite being such a major feature of our current winter landscape, the geese have deserted the area before (after the Second World War) and they could again.

There is one major change to the present landscape looming and that is the large number of wind turbines that are destined for North Norfolk. While everyone wants a more environmentally friendly energy supply, opinions remain much divided about them. The amount that might cover the Norfolk countryside and the offshore waters is substantial and it will change our views of the coastline dramatically. What the effect will be to our wildlife is not yet known, but

Unsprayed field headlands and uncultivated set aside areas like this one near North Creake have provided a lifeline for much of our declining farmland flora and fauna.

it seems logical to assume that those out at sea will surely present a potentially lethal obstacle for migrating birds during adverse weather.

Such concerns perfectly illustrate how nothing should be taken for granted and how important a necessity there is for greater foresight and a need for even more attention and care to be paid to the natural environment around us. With increasing pressures from ever more visitors, more vehicles on our quiet minor roads, the constant demands of intensive agriculture, a changing climate and the threat of rising sea levels, there is a need for a determined effort by conservationists and landowners to preserve the wildlife of North Norfolk. While today's problems are different from those in the past, the work of those pioneering conservationists in what were equally difficult times in the 1800s, should be a constant reminder of what can be achieved. Their views and concerns were in a minority and were deemed by the majority to be the thoughts of eccentrics. It can be seen that thanks to their efforts, the North Norfolk they so cherished was preserved for us all to enjoy now. Today, we have the advantage of hindsight and a far greater knowledge of environmental issues, so our decisions should really be the result of positive, well considered opinions. It is up to us to leave for future generations the legacy of a highly valued natural heritage which they can be as proud of as we are.

North Norfolk's old and new; bait diggers with the offshore wind turbines in the distance.

Little egrets flying to roost at Holkham.

Bibliography

The following books are recommended for further reading and indeed many were used as a source of reference.

Anderson S. (1988) *The Grey Seal* Shire Publications Ltd.

Banham P. (editor 1964 – 1967) *Norfolk Mammal Report* Norfolk and Norwich Naturalist's Society

Banham P. (1994) *Natural History of Wells-next-the-Sea* Seapie, Wells

Beebee T. and Griffiths R. (2000) *Amphibians and Reptiles* Harper Collins Publishers Ltd.

Beckett G. and Bull A. (1999) *A Flora of Norfolk* Gillian Beckett

Bishop B. and B. (1996) *Cley Marsh and its Birds* Hill House Press

Bloomfield A. (1993) *Birds of the Holkham Area* Andrew Bloomfield

Brooks S. and Lewington R. (1999) *Field Guide to the Dragonflies of Great Britain and Ireland* British Wildlife Publishing

Buczacki S. (2002) *Fauna Britannica* Hamlyn

Clarke R. (1995) *The Marsh Harrier* Hamlyn

Chestney B. (1993) *Island of Terns* Quiller Press

Chinery M. (1993) *Insects of Britain and Western Europe* Collins

Cocker M. and Mabey R. (2005) *Birds Britannica* Chatto and Windus

Crawford P. (1986) *The Living Isles* Book Club Associates

Cringle P. *Saltmarsh and Sandunes* Wells and District Wildfowler's Club

Dunmore G. (editor 1998 – 2007) *Norfolk Bird Report* Norfolk and Norwich Naturalists Society

Eales T. (1986) *Countryman's Memoirs* Jim Baldwin Publishing

Gantlett S. (1989) *The Birds of Cley* S.J.M. Gantlett

George M. (2000) *Birds in Norfolk and The Law, Past and Present* Norfolk and Norwich Naturalists Society

Goldsmith J. (editor 1968 – 1972) *Norfolk Mammal Report* Norfolk and Norwich Naturalist's Society

Gooden R. (1978) *British Butterflies* David and Charles Ltd.

Hancy R. (editor 1975 – 1994) *Norfolk Mammal Report* Norfolk and Norwich Naturalist's Society

Harrop A. and S. (2005) *Orchids of Britain and Ireland* A & C Black Publishers Ltd.

Harrop S. (2005) *Flowers of the Norfolk Coast* Norfolk Nature

Jonsonn L. (1992) *Birds of Europe with North Africa and the Middle East* Christopher Helm

Knights C. (2002) *The Feather and the Furrow* Bird's Farm Books

Mabey R. (1996) *Flora Britannica* Sinclair-Stevenson

Mason J. (2005) *The Hare* Merlin Unwin Books

McCallum J. (1999) *North Norfolk Wildlife Through The Seasons* Arlequin Press

McCallum J. (2001) *Wild Goose Winter* Silver Brant

McCallum J. (2003) *North Norfolk Summer Sketchbook* Silver Brant

McCallum (2006) *Larks and Leverets* Silver Brant

Nethersole-Thompson (1986) *Waders their breeding, haunts and watchers* T & A D Poyser

North D. and Hayward Smith M. (2004) *Elements of the North Norfolk Coast* Birdseyeview Books

Pashley H. (1992) *Notes on the Birds of Cley* Christopher Frost

Pearson B. and Burton R. (1991) *Birdscape* HarperCollins

Perrow M. (editor 1995 – 1998) *The Norfolk Mammal Report* Norfolk and Norwich Naturalist's Society

Seago. M (1953 – 1997) *Norfolk Bird Report* Norfolk and Norwich Naturalists Society

Scott I. (editor 2005) *Turn of the Tide: North Norfolk's Saltmarsh Coast* Quiller Publishing Ltd.